SECRET
LONGINGS
of the
HEART

SECRET LONGINGS

of the

HEART

OVERCOMING DEEP DISAPPOINTMENT AND
UNFULFILLED EXPECTATIONS

CAROL KENT

NAVPRESS®

Bringing Truth to Life

OUR GUARANTEE TO YOU

We believe so strongly in the message of our books that we are making this quality guarantee to you. If for any reason you are disappointed with the content of this book, return the title page to us with your name and address and we will refund to you the list price of the book. To help us serve you better, please briefly describe why you were disappointed. Mail your refund request to: NavPress, P.O. Box 35002, Colorado Springs, CO 80935.

NavPress
P.O. Box 35001
Colorado Springs, Colorado 80935

The Navigators is an international Christian organization. Our mission is to reach, disciple, and equip people to know Christ and to make Him known through successive generations. We envision multitudes of diverse people in the United States and every other nation who have a passionate love for Christ, live a lifestyle of sharing Christ's love, and multiply spiritual laborers among those without Christ.

NavPress is the publishing ministry of The Navigators. NavPress publications help believers learn biblical truth and apply what they learn to their lives and ministries. Our mission is to stimulate spiritual formation among our readers.

NAVPRESS, BRINGING TRUTH TO LIFE, and the NAVPRESS logo are registered trademarks of NavPress. Absence of ® in connection with marks of NavPress or other parties does not indicate an absence of registration of those marks.

ISBN 1-57683-360-7

Cover design by David Carlson Design
Cover illustration PhotoDisc/Lawrence M. Sawyer
Creative Team: Nanci McAlister, Karen Lee-Thorp, Darla Hightower, Pat Miller

Some of the anecdotal illustrations in this book are true to life and are included with the permission of the persons involved. All other illustrations are composites of real situations, and any resemblance to people living or dead is coincidental.

Unless otherwise identified, all Scripture quotations in this publication are taken from the HOLY BIBLE: NEW INTERNATIONAL VERSION® (NIV®). Copyright © 1973, 1978, 1984 by International Bible Society. Used by permission of Zondervan Publishing House. All rights reserved. Other versions used include: the *King James Version* (KJV).

Kent, Carol, 1947-
    Secret longings of the heart : overcoming deep disappointment and
unfulfilled expectations / Carol Kent.
        p. cm.
Includes bibliographical references.
    ISBN 1-57683-360-7
    1. Christian women--Religious life. 2. Emotions--Religious
aspects--Christianity. I. Title.
    BV4527 .K449 2003
    248.8'43--dc21
                                    2002152477

Printed in the United States of America

1 2 3 4 5 6 7 8 9 10 / 08 07 06 05 04 03

FOR A FREE CATALOG OF
NAVPRESS BOOKS & BIBLE STUDIES,
CALL 1-800-366-7788 (USA)
OR 1-416-499-4615 (CANADA)

Contents

❧ ❧

Acknowledgments

With deep appreciation and heartfelt gratitude I acknowledge:

MY PARENTS, CLYDE AND PAULINE AFMAN

You are my constant encouragers and prayer supporters. I thank God for your involvement in my ministry.

MY SON, JASON PAUL (J. P.)

Your effervescent spirit and spontaneous bursts of humor kept my heart encouraged during the long hours at the computer.

MY FRIEND DEBORAH K. JONES

You supported me throughout this project with countless hours of personal involvement. Thank you for "praying without ceasing," researching, answering my mail, taking phone calls, and proofreading the manuscript.

MY EDITOR, TRACI MULLINS

You taught me the meaning of the word *teamwork*. Coming alongside at a crucial time, you offered fresh ideas, challenging suggestions, and sound structure that gave this project the foundation it needed. In addition to being tremendously gifted as an editor, you had the ability to confront when necessary and to encourage throughout the writing process. Thank you for your friendship and professionalism.

MY SISTERS—JENNIE DIMKOFF, PAULA AFMAN, BONNIE EMMOREY, AND JOY CARLSON

You provided a combination of laughter, tears, memories, support, and loving encouragement throughout this project. Writing about secret passions of the Christian woman would have been much more difficult without experiencing life with my four *passionate* sisters.

MY PRAYER SUPPORTERS—KAY JELINEK, MAUREEN O'NEILL, SUSANNE RAYNER, AND MARILYN FENNER

You kept me going when I was tempted to give up. Thank you for supporting me in many tangible ways during the months of writing. You are loved!

PART ONE

Passions:
What Are They and
Where Do They Come From?

Hidden Longings of the Heart:
Recognizing the Passions
That Drive Us

All my longings lie open before you, O Lord;
my sighing is not hidden from you.

PSALM 38:9

A COUPLE OF years ago a friend of mine came for a visit. Deb is single, goal-oriented, highly motivated, and very creative. During the course of our conversation, she posed a most intriguing question: "Carol, what makes you weep and pound the table?"

I was taken aback for a moment. What a strange question. What *does* make me weep and pound the table? I asked for a more specific explanation of what she meant.

With growing intensity, she went on: "What do you feel *passionate* about?" My mind started spinning. *Passion* was a word I enjoyed using and secretly thought I possessed, but now I wasn't even sure I could properly define what it meant. That day, a one-hour lunch with a friend turned into a four-hour discussion about hopes and dreams, expectations and disappointments, longings and emotions, inner drives and resulting actions.

During the course of the afternoon, some heavy-duty brainstorming took place as Deb probed deeply: "What are the *causes, emotions, concerns, problems, people,* and *projects* you feel deeply about?" I soon realized that what I feel deeply about (even on the unconscious level) drastically affects my actions.

She continued, "What does your heart *long* to be involved in? What are your *secret dreams* for the future?" By this time my creativity was flowing and I began communicating at a deeper level, revealing things that passing acquaintances might find too lofty, too imaginative, or even amusing.

After quite some time had passed, I thought the hard questions were over, but I was wrong—Deb was just getting warmed up! "Where are you hurting right now," she asked, "and how does pain affect your perspective?" That was a tough question. I was just coming through a prolonged period of physical pain and my usual optimistic attitude had long since worn thin from the crippling grip of a damaged nerve. My motivation and personal productivity were greatly hindered by my lack of good health, even though my condition was temporary.

Deb's last queries hit me like well-placed bullets and punctured my spiritual conscience. "What are you willing to invest your time, your money, and your total energy toward? What emotions are you feeling that you don't want anyone else to know about?"

Those questions became the springboard for one of the most stimulating discussions I've ever had. There are moments in life when "peak-level" communication takes place and you begin speaking your secret passions out loud to another human being. That day I revealed my *hidden heartbeat.*

Thinking about hidden passions is one thing. Talking about them is another matter entirely. In addition to my positive, honorable, and spiritual passions, I had to admit I had passions that were stirred by my hurts, failures, family tensions, job problems, personality struggles, secret temptations, deep-felt desires, negative emotions, and bitter disappointments.

Once again I realized that I'm one of millions of women who struggle with life's complexities. Every day women experience opportunities that have the potential to lift them to glorious, stimulating joy, or plunge them into self-pity and depression. The word *passion* is as complex as the human mind. It's derived from old French and Latin roots, which mean "suffering, pain, or some disorder of body or spirit." It's also defined as "any kind of *feeling* by which the mind is powerfully affected or moved."[1]

Today, passion has strongly paradoxical meanings. It can mean any of the emotions (such as hate, grief, love, fear, or joy). It can also refer to an extreme, compelling emotional drive or excitement, such as: (a) great anger, rage, or fury; (b) enthusiasm or fondness; (c) strong love or affection; or (d) sexual drive or desire, including lust.

For the Christian woman, *passion* also has to do with living for a cause that matters. It's the perspective that no matter what unfair negatives we face, no matter what great personal tragedies come into our lives, *there is something more important to look forward to and invest our energies toward.*

WHERE DO SECRET PASSIONS COME FROM?

All of us experience emotional stress and spiritual conflict because of a great dichotomy that stems from birth. These tensions exist because of two basic facts:

Women (and men) are created in the image of God. Genesis 1:27 states, "So God created man in his own image, in the image of God he created him; male and female he created them." Natural man (woman), created in God's image, has tremendous potential—intellectually, artistically, and socially. She has a mind and body fashioned after her Maker's.

As a result, there is an inborn, natural inclination to live as she was created to live—for God's glory, using her individual creativity to make the world a better place and to develop intimate, meaningful relationships with other people. *But . . .*

Sin entered the human race in the Garden of Eden. Eve listened to the

Serpent's (Satan's) lie and thought she might be missing something wonderful. She ate of the forbidden fruit, a sin that ultimately resulted in (wo)man's separation from God. Alienation from God seems like harsh punishment for such a sin. All this trouble brought upon the human race because of *one bite?* What kind of a God would curse the earth and banish His people from paradise because they ate a little piece of fruit?

All of this makes sense if we understand these things:

- God exists.
- God has a character.
- God's character is holy (totally without sin).
- We are born sinners because of what happened in the Garden of Eden.
- God's sinless character cannot coexist with sinful people.
- For reconciliation to take place between God and man, we must admit we are sinners, agree that sin must be punished, believe Christ's substitutionary death on the cross was sufficient to free us from condemnation, and believe that He rose from the dead.
- To be born into the family of God, we must, by faith, accept all of the above as truth.

WHAT DOES THIS HAVE TO DO WITH MY PASSIONS?

We *have a sinful nature at war with our spiritual nature, even after we have accepted Christ as Savior.* We soon discover that our sinful nature tends to pervert and distort our purpose. The sin in our lives (and the sin we see in other people) inevitably leads to the frustration of our highest calling. That calling is to live like Christ, totally free and one with the Father, much like Adam and Eve were *before* the Fall.

This frustration may not be consciously felt, but it nevertheless produces conscious disappointment and pain, which in turn creates a desire for change—personally and in our world. In other words, unfulfilled expectations lead to *disappointment,* which in turn leads to *longings for change* or restoration. Our longings spark *emotion,* which fuels our *ruling passion.* Ultimately, passion leads to determined *action.*

What are *passions?* A basic definition is, "emotional responses to the disappointment of our expectations." What determines their power for good or evil is our belief system. It is natural to long for change when we are disappointed, but when our passions drive us toward personal relief more than toward honoring God and others, our actions can be destructive.

HOW CAN I CONTROL MY PASSIONS?

There is nothing worse than a sense of being out of control. Most of us want other people to think of us as rational, intelligent, spiritually motivated women who *always* act out our emotions in a controlled, Christlike fashion. But only rarely do we fit that description! Our actions are based on our conscious or unconscious belief system and can be positive, godly responses or negative, destructive responses.

Understanding the source of our passions and fully recognizing that they are a power source for good or evil will help us make some key decisions. We need to establish a belief system that can "take the heat" and help us to make right choices.

How does this work? My friend Ginny's experience provides a good illustration.

GINNY'S STORY

"I had already planned the murder in my mind. I knew *exactly* how I would execute it. I wanted to inflict pain. I wanted to mutilate. I wanted to kill. I wanted to *destroy* the man who hurt my daughters. I would have carried out my plan and I'd be in prison today if two thousand miles had not separated me from Jim."

In total shock I looked across the table at my friend. Her face was familiar, but everything else was different. I hadn't seen Ginny for several years and I could hardly believe what she was saying. Prior to this conversation, if I'd been asked to list the most gentle, sensitive, loving Christian women I'd ever met, Ginny would have been on the list. Now my mind scrambled to recall Ginny's incredible story of survival. I knew her ex-husband, Jim, had been very physically abusive, especially when he had been drinking. She never talked much about Jim, but her terrible fear of this man had been obvious to close friends. Ginny had been battered physically and verbally on numerous occasions, but she stayed with her husband, praying for a miracle.

For fifteen years she had tried to salvage what was left of the marriage. Ginny felt false pride and shame about the stubborn decision she had made to marry this man. She feared divorce would affect her relationship with God. But there were two young daughters to protect. One day while Jim was in a drunken rage, he lunged at her with a knife in his hand; she knew then it was time to leave and take her precious daughters with her.

Ginny's voice brought me back to the present. "You know, Carol, my daughters are grown now. They are beautiful, compassionate, and intelligent young women, and they have brought me joy even during the most discouraging days of my life. Last year they flew in to visit me. While the girls were in town, we were invited to have dinner in the home of dear friends. Following the meal, our conversation turned to past events and future goals; we shared openly and then we went on to a time of prayer."

Struggling to control her emotions, Ginny continued her story. "During the prayer time, both of my girls began weeping uncontrollably. I put my arms around them and one of them said, 'Mom, we can't keep the secret any longer. We feel so dirty. Can God ever forgive us? After your divorce from Daddy, when it was his weekend to have us, he would drink and then force himself on Jody and me. He had sex with us almost every time it was his turn for visitation. Maybe we could have stopped him, but we didn't know what to do. We love Dad, but he was always so different when he was drinking. We feel like we've sinned against God. Will we ever quit feeling so dirty?'"

Ginny paused, and with fire in her eyes she stated, "Carol, until that moment I didn't know I was capable of feeling such an intense level of hatred. Anger and desire for vengeance flooded over me as I comprehended the reality of my worst fear: My little girls, who were only ten and eleven years old at the time, had been repeatedly sexually abused by their own father! Rage seared through my veins, but this time it was directed at God. Where was He when this happened?"

Ginny took a deep breath and explained more of this horror story. While listening to her girls that night, she mentally devised a plan for killing the man who had brought her children such heartfelt pain and undeserved guilt.

Ginny spoke haltingly as she related the story of her lengthy personal battle to forgive her ex-husband for such a heinous crime. She carried intense anger at God for a full year. She hated the dryness in her relationship with the Lord, but her disappointment and anger outweighed her desire for change. One day, with her emotions warring within, she fell to her knees. By faith, not feeling, she poured her heart out to God. Jody and Karen were beside her and she voiced her prayer aloud.

"Dear God," Ginny began. "In myself I cannot speak the words, but in Your strength I ask for help. Lord, *by faith* I forgive Jim for sexually abusing my young daughters and for making them live with such a horrible guilt-producing secret all of these years. Father, I cannot do this apart from You. Take away the guilt and the hatred. Free my girls from the painful memories of the past. Replace this horror with Your love. Give them healing and mental rest. Grant them spiritual wholeness. Forgive me for my wicked, murderous thoughts toward this man. Oh, God, I thank You for hearing me today and for giving me Your peace. Amen."

How Ginny Controlled Her Passions

Ginny's story does not have an ending yet. I have not told her story for the purpose of offering a quick-fix solution or to suggest that deeply hidden passions—such as murderous thoughts—can be instantly controlled with one sincere prayer. None of us will experience the absence of all pain until we reach heaven. To pretend that hurt isn't there or that life is perfect "now that we're right with God" would be to deny that we live in a fallen world with unfulfilled longings, disappointments, abuse, lust, hunger, pain, confusion, and at times more questions than answers.

But if we look more closely at what happened in Ginny's mind and heart as she responded to her circumstances, we can see a clear process at work that enabled her to redirect her murderous impulses.

Ginny's Expectation: That she would have a happy Christian marriage and would raise two lovely daughters in a positive environment until they were able to be on their own as productive, contributing members of society.

Ginny's Disappointment: Her marriage was a failure and her daughters were sexually abused by their own father. Consequently, her daughters had the potential of being negatively affected for life in their personal relationships.

Ginny's Longing: This great disappointment stirred a mixture of deep longings within Ginny for change or restoration. One longing was that she and her daughters would *never* have to see Jim again and that he would never be allowed to see them again. Another longing was an intense desire to protect her daughters and to "fix" any damage that had been done to them.

Ginny's Emotions: Her longings immediately brought violent emotions—in this case, anger and hatred directed at Jim that resulted in murderous thoughts. She wanted to inflict slow, agonizing pain with the same intensity she and her daughters had experienced.

Ginny's Belief System: Up until this point, Ginny's responses were morally neutral. But a decision had to be made regarding what to do with those negative emotions. Because there was a great physical distance between her and her ex-husband, Ginny spent a considerable amount of time sifting her poignant feelings through the grid of her personal convictions. Ginny is a Christian who has a strong system of values based on the Bible. After she analyzed her sharply painful emotions in the light of her relationship with God, her knowledge of His Word, and her intense love for her daughters, the decision finally was made.

Ginny's Ruling Passion: If she had valued relief more than anything else, Ginny's drive (ruling passion) would have been revenge. That passion would have produced vengeful action toward Jim! But Ginny made a different decision. Above all else she valued obeying God, and she knew His will was for her to forgive. Her ruling passion, therefore, resulted in an action of Christlike behavior.

Ginny's Action: When a decision is made regarding a ruling passion, the final action will be directed toward good or evil. For Ginny, the action of prayer was required, asking God for the grace to develop and display forgiveness in her life.

If Ginny had not stopped to consider her values in the light of God's, or if she had denied what she most deeply longed for (which actually was to be God's woman), she might have let her natural, sinful bent drive her to destruction. One of her major longings was to protect her daughters and help them to be emotionally healed. After considering her deep desire to choose to be God's woman, her fiery passion cooled in an action of forgiveness and an ongoing involvement in nurturing her daughters.

LET'S GET HONEST

This is a book about facing secret passions. Each chapter will identify a different hidden longing that—consciously or unconsciously—fuels our passions. Many different longings provide kindling for the fire of passions.

We have longings *to possess* things that are out of our reach. We experience longings *to escape* difficult life situations. Some of us deeply desire *to transform* our lives from the inside out. Others of us want *to transcend* daily circumstances and live out our real purpose. And all of us long *to matter* to somebody else, to feel significant.

Our longings can result in ruling passions and actions that are destructive, honorable, or holy. This book is written for women who desire to learn the secret of handling the disappointment of their unfulfilled expectations in the right way so their ruling passions will be powerful forces for good rather than evil.

The requirements for getting the most out of this book are rigorous honesty and careful responses to the following questions:

- What are the aches in my heart that have never been touched?
- Do I have hidden negative emotions that have been covered over with denial or feverish work?
- Is there anyone I dislike, hate, envy, resent, or fear?
- What are my secrets?
- Do I understand God's answers to my hidden longings?
- What are my expectations of myself and my world?
- How do I usually handle my disappointments?

Why should we be in touch with the deepest parts of ourselves? The greatest benefit is that we can begin making conscious, God-honoring decisions about our present and our future, rather than being driven blindly by our emotions. In the next chapter we'll get started by evaluating our own longings, which fuel the passions behind our actions.

CHAPTER 2

Secret Passions—Destructive, Honorable, or Holy?: Recognizing the Sources of Passion

*I turned my mind to understand, to investigate
and to search out wisdom.*
ECCLESIASTES 7:25

ALL OF us have passions. These drives, fed by our longings, are often kept in a secret place, far from the knowledge of other people— and even ourselves. Sometimes these secret passions are fueled by strong negative emotions, such as Ginny experienced when she was filled with hurt and anger over the abuse of her daughters. When the emotion rages, the secret passion becomes common knowledge as actions are carried out.

Passions can be based on a deep longing to escape our present circumstances. Or they can be produced by an intense desire to have something out of reach. Passion is the fuel that produces major changes in our lifestyle, behavior, and attitudes. Ultimately, passions can give us the energy to live out our real purpose in life and see the big picture.

Occasionally secret passions are fiercely spiritual. These passions drive us to work for a creed, cause, or desired outcome that is high and holy.

These passions are often based on our longings to live out the purpose we were created for and to use our best gifts for a worthy cause.

HOW DO UNCONSCIOUS PASSIONS DRIVE US?

Life goes by swiftly. Our days are filled with making a living, interacting with people, responding to emergencies, fulfilling obligations, keeping pace with current demands, eating, sleeping, and personal hygiene. That leaves little time to stop long enough to think about *why* we do what we do.

A young woman told me she had struggled for the past four years with a severe eating disorder. She explained her cycle of bingeing on enormous amounts of food, then purging through inducing vomiting and abusing laxatives. Lori was slender, attractive, and educated. My first thought was, *Why would someone like this have a problem like that?*

After a while I asked, "Lori, do you know why you first started this cycle of bingeing and purging?"

She immediately responded. "Because I wanted to look good to other people. It was simply a way of controlling my weight when I desired food that had too many calories. I guess I felt I had no self-control."

As we moved deeper into the discussion, she told me her mother had always been substantially overweight and her father used to joke about her fat in demeaning ways, often in front of other people. He would frequently pinch her mother's extra flesh along the ribs or move her saggy, heavy arms back and forth while making derogatory comments. Lori always felt like crying when this happened, but to her dad, it was always a humorous matter.

Lori's father was demanding in many ways; she was afraid to bring home her report card for fear he would be disappointed with a "B+" grade instead of an "A." He was slow to praise, and even as a young adult Lori admitted she was still trying to be good enough to please him.

It soon became obvious to me why Lori had severe bulimia. Her present dilemma had resulted from a series of subconscious decisions based on disappointed longings that fed her passion and finally produced destructive action. Let's take a look at how it happened.

Lori's Expectation: That her father would love her, affirm her, and be pleased with her; that he would love, verbally affirm, and be pleased with her mother.

Lori's Disappointment: Through the years, no matter how hard her mother tried to please her husband (Lori's father), he was still relentless with his hurtful criticism. Likewise, Lori discovered it was impossible to do anything well enough to earn her father's approval.

Lori's Longing: Her deep disappointment led to a desire for change. In Lori's case, her true longing was for unbridled, nonjudgmental, Christlike love from her father that would be directed toward her and her mother, regardless of their physical appearances or performance. Lori did not fully understand this longing, and she continued to try to find a way to be acceptable to her dad.

Lori's Emotions: Lori's emotions included a *zeal* to be thin enough to win her father's acceptance and a *fear* of ridicule, embarrassment, and rejection if she ever became overweight.

Lori's Belief System: She knew (intellectually) that God loved her and that she was important to Him no matter how much she weighed, but her values system had become distorted by years of unsuccessfully trying to please her father and by watching her mother crumble under his incessant criticism. The damage to her emotions and thinking processes made relief (soothing her pain by controlling her body) her highest priority—and her actions reflected that choice.

Lori's Ruling Passion: If Lori's values had been tied securely to the authority of God's Word, if she'd been convinced of her unalterable worth to her Father in heaven, her ruling passion could have become devotion to Him. Because her values were unclear and her deepest longings unacknowledged, her instinctive drive was to be physically attractive—no matter what the cost.

Lori's Action: The cost for Lori was bondage to a severe eating disorder.

SECRET PASSIONS

Our secret passions have their roots in deep longings within—desires we think about regularly but often avoid declaring openly. Most of us don't talk about our secret passions, since we're convinced no one else could possibly empathize with our unique situation in life. It's often easier for us to hide our true feelings than to risk rejection or ridicule.

These hidden passions are also formed by the subconscious longings we are too busy to recognize or too hurt to admit. Sometimes we're aware of our longings but not in touch with the emotions they spark. If Lori had known she longed for her father's approval, but hadn't been aware of how hurt, angry, fearful, and even ashamed she felt over not receiving approval, then knowing her longings wouldn't have done her any good. So it's vital that we understand the connection between our longings and our emotions that lead us to action.

Hidden passions are difficult to direct as a power source for good because it's much easier to exist in a comfortable rut than risk vulnerability and talk to someone about our personal need. *By not being in touch with our longings and emotions, we lose the ability to make conscious decisions about our present and future and end up living by our emotions.*

Hidden longings reveal the *real* person inside of us as they feed the passions that drive us. According to Proverbs 23:7 (KJV), "As [a man] thinketh in his heart, so is he."

PASSIONS—DESTRUCTIVE, HONORABLE, OR HOLY?

In the first chapter we mentioned that our ruling passions are determined by our belief system and can be characterized in any of the following three ways.

DESTRUCTIVE

Destructive passions destroy a person's potential for happiness, personal productivity, and spiritual fulfillment.

Example: A Christian mother expects that her son will one day become an adult with an opportunity for marriage, a good job, and a family. Her son is killed at age sixteen by a drunk driver. This mother longs to have her son back. Since that isn't possible, her longing for change turns to the driver of the vehicle. She wants him to pay for what he did by serving time in prison and having his driver's license revoked permanently. This mother's initial emotion is anger toward the driver and a deep desire for revenge. Thoughts of God are far from her at the moment. With a distorted belief system, she makes her decision. Her ruling passion becomes an intense drive to constantly relive the details of the accident and verbalize fitting punishments for the driver. Her twisted action makes the people around her miserable. The result for this woman is bitterness, poor health, and depression; but she does not view her passion as a sin or a problem needing attention.

HONORABLE

Honorable passions bring energy and enthusiasm to uplifting and worthwhile relationships, causes, and projects.

Example: A young woman had a sister who was born with cystic fibrosis. She watched as her sister Dayna struggled with a terminal illness that allowed her enough healthy periods to significantly impact her world with numerous personal contributions. Dayna blessed others with her contagious sense of humor, watercolor paintings, challenging conversation, and deep loyalty in friendships. Serious symptoms of the disease periodically flared up with no advance notice, leaving Dayna with severe breathing and digestive problems. When Dayna died, her passing seemed premature. There were so many things she wanted to accomplish, so many hopes and dreams left unfulfilled.

Her sister, propelled by a passion that had God's interests at heart, took up the cause of making the Cystic Fibrosis Foundation a major focus of her energy. Instead of wasting precious time mourning indefinitely for a sister who was gone, she devoted several hours a week to fund-raising and making speeches that motivated the search for a cure for this dreadful disease.

HOLY

Holy passions bring about fulfillment of the Great Commission—leading people to Christ and leading young Christians to maturity through instruction.

Example: A. Wetherell Johnson, an English-born missionary to China, was put in a Japanese internment camp near Shanghai during World War II. When released, she was in poor health and was robbed of her former place of ministry. Already in her fifties, she went to California to recuperate.

Instead of settling into retirement with every possibility of feeling bitter and resentful for being thrown into a prison camp, thrust out of a mission field, and besieged with poor health, she saw a new opportunity to minister to a handful of women. She started a home Bible study that soon moved to a church because of the number of women who came. People in other cities asked her to start Bible studies in their areas, and within a few short years Miss Johnson founded what is now called Bible Study Fellowship.

Today, thousands of men and women study her Bible study notes in weekly classes held around the globe. Countless people have been won to Christ and receive regular instruction from the Word of God as a result of one woman's holy passion.

Upon release from the prison camp, Miss Johnson stated, "Your deepest joy comes when you have nothing around you to bring outward pleasure and Jesus becomes your total joy."[1] Miss Johnson's values determined how she handled her disappointments and they became the energy behind her holy passion.

WHAT LONGINGS ARE BURIED IN YOUR HEART?

My interest in this subject comes from an inner knowledge that my personal passions control me. When they are honorable and holy, wonderful things happen. People around me are encouraged and I have an inner sense of joy and deep personal fulfillment.

The problem is that more often than I'd like to admit, my passions are destructive. The reason for this is that when I dwell on my disappointments and the reality that certain things in life aren't what I expect, I long for a change. And sometimes my longings are so intense that I react solely from my emotions. I don't stop to think about what God values or how my goals line up with His. My emotions, rather than my values, drive me.

I've always been curious about why I do what I do. What drives me? Why do I work so hard for approval? Why do my disappointments spur me toward deep longings for change? If you're like me, you probably ask yourself some of the same questions.

I don't think deeply each day about what determines my actions, but I instinctively know when my behavior and attitudes are God-honoring or when they are destructive. My biggest purpose in writing this book is to help people like me understand how to recognize the longings that lead to passions, and to recognize them in time to control the emotions and choose the action that will exalt the Lord and help other people. We can't do it alone, but with prayer, practice, and patience, there is hope!

When the idea for this book first came to me, I interviewed women across the country about their secret passions. Their gut-level honesty and surprisingly frank responses to my questions helped me to identify certain kinds of longings that form the bedrock of passion—passion that can be constructive or destructive, concealed or celebrated. In each case, there is a choice. Will the action that is motivated by the longing be destructive, honorable, or holy? Maybe you, like me, have experienced some of the same disappointments that produce the following five types of longings.

In the following examples, the places, names, and a few significant details are changed to protect the anonymity of the individuals who shared their stories. As you read each story, ask yourself what longings are buried in your heart and how your longings have produced your ruling passions.

FIVE TYPES OF LONGINGS

1. LONGING TO MATTER (TO HAVE IMPACT AND SIGNIFICANCE)

- "I was the fifth daughter born in my family. From the time I was very small, it was obvious that my father had been wanting a son—probably since the first girl was born. Two years later he got his wish and my brother was born. Dad played ball with Billy and took him hunting. There were lots of baby pictures of Billy, but almost none of me. Even though my basic needs of food, clothing, and shelter were met, I never felt special to my father. All my life I've wanted him to be proud of me and to enjoy spending time with me, but that's never happened."

- "For years I have been calling a woman regularly to talk about all my troubles and to ask for her advice. I would like to have her as a friend, but I don't feel good enough about myself to feel worthy of that kind of a relationship. I'm really afraid that if I didn't have personal struggles and concerns to bring up on the phone, she'd wonder why someone like me would be calling her."

2. LONGING TO POSSESS (TO HAVE SOMETHING OUT OF REACH)

- "All I have ever wanted is a baby of my own. I have had five miscarriages, and every time I see a happy mother holding her infant, part of me cries and the other part gets angry at God. *Why* would He withhold from me that which I want most? It isn't fair!"

- "I'll turn forty this year and my husband and I have never owned a home of our own. We have worked harder than most couples; we've always tried to budget, but we have *never* been out of debt. Last year the car fell apart and had to be replaced. This year we had unexpected medical expenses. There's always something that keeps us from our deep longing for financial security, and the stress is more than I can bear."

- "When God made me, He must have run out of good building material. I have exercised consistently for the last three years, but I'm still too short, too round, and too plain. My skin is pitted from teenage acne, and I have never felt beautiful for even one day of my life."

- "Every day I ask God for a husband, and I haven't had a date in two years. I long for someone to hold me tenderly. I'm not asking for a movie star. A regular, average, kind, loving man would do. I am so lonely I could die."

- "I was passed over for the position I'm most qualified for, and now I'm stuck in a dead-end job that requires none of my creativity. I'm bored, unhappy, depressed, and unfulfilled. I need my paycheck for survival and see no hope for getting out of the rut."

3. Longing to Escape (to be released from bondage)

- "I married the best-looking guy in the world! He was the strong, silent type and there was something about his slow speech that gave him an aura of mystery and intrigue. Now we've been married for ten years and I'm wondering why. If he isn't buried in the newspaper, he's engrossed in a television sports event. He will not communicate, and he has no concept of how cutoff I feel. I wish there was a way to gracefully leave this marriage and find someone to give me the companionship my heart desires."

- "Working in my profession is one of the opportunities of a lifetime! It's fulfilling, challenging, mentally and spiritually stimulating, and they *pay* me to do it. The only trouble is that the more I work, the more there is to do. My work possesses my mind from the moment I get up to the minute I lie down. I wake up in the night and can't get back to sleep because creative ideas are swirling in my head. I seem incapable of *balancing* my life so that my inner drive to accomplish 'important' work is kept in proper perspective without holding me in bondage to it."

- "My greatest internal struggle is with my fantasies. I long to be cherished, and my husband isn't meeting that need. When I meet charming Christian men, I inevitably think about being in their arms and making love with someone who would make me feel beautiful and desirable. I have confessed this sin to God repeatedly, but the thoughts always come back."

- "If I could be released from anger, I could be a good Christian woman. My mother has been overprotective since the day I was born. She never allowed me to make my own decisions, and she saw my emerging independence as a threat. Now I'm in my mid-thirties and she's still controlling my life. Just last week she told me to quit wearing eye shadow because it makes me look like a prostitute. I can't believe she is *still* capable of reducing me to tears and manipulating my emotions like this. Just seeing her enter a room makes me so angry I could scream!"

4. LONGING TO TRANSFORM (TO CHANGE FROM THE INSIDE OUT)
  - "While I'm smiling on the outside, I'm struggling with jealousy on the inside. So many women have an easier life than I do, and envy is starting to take root. Each day I mentally list what I dislike about my circumstances and I'm always wishing I could be confident and happy like other people."

  - "I was born with a negative attitude. In spite of being raised in a good home with encouraging parents, I have always tended to criticize before praising. Sometimes I can't believe the harsh tone of my voice and the demeaning speech that comes out of my mouth. I wish I could be a more positive person."

5. LONGING TO TRANSCEND

(TO SEE THE BIGGER PICTURE AND LIVE OUT MY REAL PURPOSE)

- "There's a spiritual dimension to my life that longs to make a tangible difference in this world. When I read stories of moral injustice in the world, I'm ready to sign a petition or make a speech to defend the just and to stand up for what's right. I have a burning passion to see the Supreme Court decision on abortion reversed. If it means money, time, or personal commitment, I will do whatever it takes to bring the truth to the forefront and defend innocent victims."

- "My husband and I live in a house with mud walls and a mud floor. When we married I didn't know that we would become missionaries in Bolivia. The roaches are so big here, they began eating up our wedding gifts. The heat, humidity, and bugs are often our greatest discouragements, but we are driven by one supreme desire—to bring the message of salvation to the native tribes of Bolivia. We will not give up because our eyes are on the goal of reaching men and women with the truth of God's love."

THE NEXT STEP

One of the first steps to Christian growth is to identify our hidden longings. Are they drawing us closer to God or pulling us away from Him? The next few chapters will help us explore our inner chambers. Each of us has deep longings for significance, security, intimacy, success, and spirituality. Is that wrong?

Absolutely not! God knows our longings and the emotions they spark, and He understands them. It was God Himself who placed pre-Fall expectations and desires in our hearts, and He doesn't condemn us for having feelings. He also understands the personal process we go through as we develop the passions that rule our lives, and He is always ready and willing to help us sort out our secret feelings and thoughts—even the ones that don't seem "right."

When we *own* our personal passions and stand before Him, all pretense is dropped and one by one we can evaluate our inner longings, emotions, and motives in the light of His holiness. That sounds like a big order, but God wants us to recognize our passions for what they are, acknowledge their potential power, and channel them in the right direction.

It's motivating for me to realize that my secret passions can be a tremendous source of power for getting God's work accomplished in this world. By acknowledging and evaluating our passions, we can discover how to lead a much more honest, focused, fulfilling, and purposeful life— a life based on eternal values.

Instead of feeling ashamed or threatened by our emotions, we can pass them through the grid of a belief system based on the Word of God so our passions and ultimately our actions will be for our good, the good of others, and the good of God's kingdom. I really want that to be true in my life, and it all starts with gut-level honesty. Let's get started!

PART TWO

The Passion
for Significance

CHAPTER 3

I Want to Feel Special:
To Know Whose I Am

I'm Nobody! Who are you?
Are you—Nobody too?
Then there's a pair of us! Don't tell!
They'd advertise—you know.[1]
EMILY DICKINSON, 1861

EMPTY. ALONE. Hurting. I could see the young woman out of the corner of my eye. She was strategically moving through the crowd toward me, pressing against clumps of people gathered into randomly placed conversation clusters in the small room. Her sallow, anxious face told a story without words. She had problems in her life, and she wanted to talk to somebody—anybody who would listen.

Glancing at the clock and knowing time pressures were great, I discreetly scanned the room for the closest exit. By moving quickly, I could safely remove myself from the possibility of getting into a lengthy discussion with the nameless woman. Turning to go, I found myself face-to-face with an eager conference participant. She bubbled with enthusiasm and thanked me for speaking. After chatting momentarily, I proceeded toward the door to make my escape.

Within two feet of freedom, I felt a tug on my arm. Turning around, my eyes momentarily met those of my pursuer. She haltingly stammered, "I know you probably don't have much time, but could we talk for a moment before you leave? In your message today . . . " She hesitated again, trying to express her thoughts. I could feel myself pulling away, stepping slowly toward the door, avoiding serious eye contact, and casually glancing at my watch while simultaneously feigning interest in this woman's need.

She read my body language as easily as if it had been shouted through a megaphone. Backing off, she mumbled, "Oh, never mind. I know you're busy. It was nothing anyway. Thank you for coming today."

Caught! Guilty! Convicted! The words were reverberating like a hammer in my conscience, reminding me that my subtle "pulling away" from this woman had just negated everything I had said in my presentation about how significant we are to God and how, in turn, we should practice the example of Jesus.

I had carefully reminded the listeners of the necessity to look closely at the life of Christ recorded in the gospels and notice the way He responded to people. When He looked at individuals, He had kind eyes and empathy. He had a way of looking people in the eye and nonverbally communicating that they were important, valued, and singly significant.

And He touched them. I described Him moving through the crowds with focused eye contact, picking out people who were lonely and felt unworthy, and reaching out with a touch to communicate hope and love to them.

I had carefully pointed out that everywhere He went, Jesus gave people a sense of identity and worthiness. He practiced body language that made people feel accepted and special. Throughout the gospels we read that *Jesus looked at people with eyes of compassion,* and *He touched them.*

Stabbed with a pang of guilt, I went after the woman and found a quiet place to talk. I was initially surprised by her lack of focused eye contact.

For someone who had desired this meeting so much, she appeared unable to look at me for longer than an instant; then her gaze would go to the floor, to her lap, or to the wall. Without words, her behavior made a strong statement. She had no self-worth, and it had been a monumental act of courage for her to approach me.

She spoke with measured caution. "I'm Meg. I'm nobody special, and I shouldn't be taking your time, but I had to talk to somebody. . . . "

THE BASIC TRUTH

I was born with a need to feel significant. You were, too! We need to know that we are important to someone else. If you were born in a home where your worth was questioned, you have no doubt struggled for a lifetime to discover a sense of *belonging*.

If, however, you were told from your earliest days that you are a uniquely special human being, you may feel good about yourself. The real problem is that most of us question our worth regularly, even if we had the most positive upbringing.

Perhaps because *feeling significant* is a lifelong battle for most of us—even for mature Christian women—we have an urgent need to know beyond any doubt that we are personally important to God and that He has something important for us to do with our time, talent, and energy.

As I already mentioned in the first chapter of this book, the Bible gives us a clear statement of our worth. Genesis 1:27 says, "So God created man in his own image, in the image of God he created him; male and female he created them." Francis Schaeffer put it this way, "God tells man who he is. God tells us that He created man in His image. So man is something wonderful."[1]

Psalm 139 tells us that we are fearfully and wonderfully made. We are reminded that God created our inmost being and knit us together in our mother's womb. We're told that our frame was not hidden from God when we were formed in the secret place and that His eyes saw our unformed body. The psalmist also states that all of the days that God ordained for us were written in His book before we were even born.

So why do we so often question our worth? Why do feelings of insignificance sometimes cloud everything the Bible says about us? Why do we sometimes let one person destroy our sense of belonging? Why do we struggle with what other people think of us?

MEG'S STORY

The woman I mentioned earlier had a story to tell. She was the fifth daughter born to her parents. Two years later her father, who had longed for a son, got his wish. The day of her brother's birth, her father came bursting into the house saying, "It's a boy! It's a boy! After all these years, I have a son!" During the Christmas holidays that year, the family sent a special picture card with news of the birth to friends and relatives.

Meg's sister Susan—child number four—was especially attractive. While Meg was young, she would often hear her parents say to guests, "Yes, Susan is the little beauty in the family."

The words stung, and Meg decided to compensate in her own way. She might not have been born beautiful, but she was smart and excelled in school. Her grades were high. Susan, on the other hand, struggled with her schoolwork. When Meg's parents saw the respective report cards, they withheld from Meg any words of praise for her outstanding grades. They feared Susan would feel badly and praise might make Meg become too full of pride.

The family picture albums confirmed to Meg that she was the unwanted child. There was an abundance of pictures of her brother, and there were numerous photos of her older sisters at play, but almost none of Meg.

During the next few years, Meg practiced two opposing lifestyles interchangeably. For a number of years, she was a workaholic, striving for top grades and scholarships, desperately seeking significance through earning the approval her heart desired. When no approval was shown, she turned inward, withdrawing from family and friends. With so many children to care for, Meg's parents didn't notice the obvious signals. They never realized how hurt and angry she was becoming. Meg made her own mental outline: (1) She was unwanted, (2) she was ugly, (3) she was shy, and (4) she wished she'd never been born.

Meg watched as her father lovingly affirmed her older sisters; he was also quick to put an arm around her brother and support him by attending all of his softball games. But when Meg received the lead part in her junior play and had practiced for months, her mother came to the production alone. Her father excused himself, saying he couldn't attend because the play was the same night as his church board meeting. Meg was gracious on the outside, but fiery emotions of deep anger and intense hurt were building on the inside like a volcano.

By the time I met Meg, she had quit school, given birth to a child out of wedlock, married a man who beat her, and had no contact with her parents. Her sense of worth was so low she found it impossible to hold her head up. She slumped like a shapeless piece of clay in the chair beside me. So far from God. So hopeless. So sad. No anticipation for the future. No sense of belonging. No knowledge of worthiness. A lone tear made its way down her cheek to the corner of her mouth. I groped for words. There was nothing in me that could quote Bible verses, pray a meaningful prayer, or tell her things would get better when she got right with God.

My own emotions were compassion and concern for the woman I'd tried to flee from one hour earlier. I put my arms around her and wept, only to find that she stiffened beneath my touch. Physical touch from a caring human being was foreign to her, and she felt uncomfortable receiving it. Could she ever know how special she was to God if her own father had never given her a sense of belonging?

UNDERSTANDING LOW SELF-ESTEEM

Meg's situation is more severe than some of us go through, but there is not a woman alive who does not understand what it feels like to be a "nobody." The universal struggle for all of us is a deep, painful yearning to know that there is *something* about us that *somebody* finds special. Physical beauty and financial security do little to keep the doubts from coming. And feeling significant for a moment in time does nothing to guarantee that questions of worth won't return.

Several years ago Dr. James Dobson described what it *feels* like for a woman to have low self-esteem:

> It is sitting alone in a house during the quiet afternoon hours, wondering why the phone doesn't ring . . . wondering why you have no "real" friends. It is longing for someone to talk to soul to soul, but knowing there is no such person worthy of your trust. It is feeling that "they wouldn't like me if they knew the real me." . . . It is wondering why other people have so much more talent and ability than you do. It is feeling incredibly ugly and sexually unattractive. It is admitting that you have become a failure as a wife and mother. It is disliking everything about yourself and wishing . . . you could be someone else. It is feeling unloved and unlovable and lonely and sad. It is lying in bed after the family is asleep, pondering the vast emptiness inside and longing for unconditional love. . . . It is reaching up in the darkness to remove a tear from the corner of your eye. It is depression![3]

Our deepest sense of significance always comes when a valued person conveys unequivocally that we are uniquely and distinctly important, personally acceptable, approved of, and profoundly wanted.

OUR LONGING FOR ACCEPTANCE

As far back as the Garden of Eden, relationships were meant to bring joy, completeness, acceptance, and significance to human beings. We were created for God's pleasure and companionship. He ordained that we should enjoy each other and that our significance would come from Him.

But Satan is a great deceiver! Not only did he destroy the perfect relationship Adam and Eve had with God, he also began strategically planting ungodly doubts in the hearts of every man and woman who has been born since that time.

The list of people who doubted how special they were reads like *Who's Who in Scripture.*

Moses: God's chosen leader of the Exodus despised his own humanity: "Who am I, that I should go to Pharaoh and bring the Israelites out of Egypt? . . . O Lord, I have never been eloquent, neither in the past nor since you have spoken to your servant. I am slow of speech and tongue. . . . O Lord, please send someone else to do it" (Exodus 3:11; 4:10,13).

Joshua: The Lord's inspiring challenge to Joshua gives us a glimpse of his insecurity: "Be strong and courageous. Do not be terrified; do not be discouraged, for the LORD your God will be with you wherever you go" (Joshua 1:9).

David: One day David sat before the Lord and thoughtfully said, "Who am I, O Sovereign LORD, and what is my family, that you have brought me this far?" (2 Samuel 7:18).

Elijah: God had just destroyed 450 prophets of Baal, but Jezebel entered the scene and "Elijah was afraid and ran for his life. . . . He came to a broom tree, sat down under it and prayed that he might die. 'I have had enough, LORD, . . . Take my life; I am no better than my ancestors'" (1 Kings 19:3-4).

Jeremiah: Could anyone have felt less adequate than Jeremiah when God told him his main job as a prophet would involve numerous and demanding responsibilities? "Ah, Sovereign LORD . . . I do not know how to speak; I am only a child" (Jeremiah 1:6).

When we think realistically about the accomplishments of these great biblical leaders, it's easy to smile and wonder how in the world they *ever* doubted their significance—especially to God! But if I look at myself honestly, I understand. If the Enemy can make me feel unloved, insignificant, worthless, alone, inadequate, and friendless, I become incapable of being a secure Christian woman who has a positive impact on my family, my work, and my ministry.

THE GREAT MYSTERY

The dynamic, successful Bible leaders mentioned in the previous section struggled with the same dilemma you and I face every day. We consistently confuse *what we do* with *who we are*. For years I worked myself to a frazzle trying to be special to God—always confusing *doing* with *being*. One day, in worn-out desperation, I shouted my sob to God, "Lord, I'm trying to be a five-talent person in a two-talent body, and I can't do it anymore!" I was suffering under the delusion that if I would say yes to every ministry opportunity that came along, I would be more special to God and to other Christian people I longed to impress.

WHAT REALLY HAPPENS?

We have an inborn expectation to feel special—to God and to other people. We were designed by God to enjoy perfect relationships in a perfect, pre-fallen world. When there is a discrepancy between our expectations and reality, disappointment sets in, causing a deep desire for change. This longing produces an initial emotion, an automatic response that screams out, "If I don't feel significant, life isn't worth living!" As we run those emotions through the grid of our belief system, a ruling passion takes over and drives us in one of two directions: one that pleases God or one that reflects our destructive thinking.

WHAT HAPPENED TO MEG

Meg's Expectation: Meg had a deep and natural expectation that she would be special to her parents, that they would see her as a valued and important part of the family.

Meg's Disappointment: Her disappointment came over a period of years as she observed her parents' attention to her pretty sister and her only brother. The disappointment was reinforced as her dramatic abilities were not given the same value as her brother's athletic achievements.

Meg's Longing: Out of her deep disappointment, Meg's longing was born: a deep desire for approval, value, respect, and worth from the people most important to her—her mom and dad!

Meg's Emotions: Hurt hardly begins to describe what Meg felt as a result of her parents' rejection. She was crushed. The little girl in her agonized over having what she most longed for completely out of reach. Her hurt and shame gave way to a boiling anger and bitterness.

Meg's Belief System: Running her painful emotions through a damaged belief system, Meg made a decision. Life devoid of affirmation from the people she loved was too painful. She didn't dare explore her unfulfilled longings in light of God's truth and discover her security and significance in Him. She had to find another way to ease her current pain.

Meg's Ruling Passion: Meg was driven by a passion for relief from her pain—at all costs. And the cost nearly destroyed her life.

Meg's Action: Meg's ruling passion drove her to seek a sense of specialness and self-worth by excelling and then by rebelling. Her initial hurt propelled her to workaholic tendencies in an effort to *earn* her parents' approval. When that didn't work, she turned her back on her Christian upbringing and decided to practice destructive, rebellious behavior in a final attempt to gain their attention.

After her initial outburst of atypical, boisterous, and inappropriate behavior, she turned inward, withdrawing from people and burying herself in depression. She became pregnant by the first man who paid attention to her and married him too quickly. His violent physical abuse caused her physical as well as emotional pain, and her distorted belief system reminded her that she was a "nothing" and probably deserved to be treated with disrespect. Meg's ungodly ruling passion propelled her into a lifestyle of sadness, depression, hopelessness, and spiritual devastation.

WHERE DO WE FIT?

Most women have far less dramatic stories than Meg, but all of us can see a part of our innermost being in her situation. If we were raised by parents who held us tenderly, who verbally affirmed our great worth, who consistently "dreamed great dreams for our future" while actively helping us to pursue those dreams, we were fortunate indeed! We probably have a very positive picture of who God is and how valuable we are to Him, too. But if we had parents who failed to love us this well (and most of us did), we may have a hard time experiencing the love of our heavenly Father. Unfortunately, we tend to view God a great deal like we view our earthly parents.

I was sitting in an audience listening to a wardrobe consultant when she pointed out the importance of honesty. Her best advice was to take a few private moments at home to lock ourselves in our bathroom, strip down to the flesh, and stand in front of a full-length mirror and itemize our assets and liabilities.

Sometimes I wish we all could do that same exercise mentally and strip down to our bare motives, longings, passions, desires, and drives. Wouldn't it be interesting to weigh our activities on a scale that could automatically tell us whether we're living in an attempt to be special to God or to other people, or whether we have discovered the truth that *who we are* in His sight is more important than *what we do?*

What a helpful tool it would be for all of us who have struggled with low self-esteem to be able to have a device that would chronologically flash a videotape of our lives on a screen and point out the critical points in life where our disappointments produced longings for change. If we could only evaluate our emotional responses *before* deciding on a negative, destructive ruling passion, we might avoid *years* of a difficult, depressing existence.

WHERE CAN SIGNIFICANCE BE FOUND?

I have always enjoyed an intellectual challenge, and one of my favorite activities continues to be "creative verbal sparring" with people who have definite opinions about religion, politics, current issues, and impossible dreams. As a firstborn, obsessive-compulsive, driven, type-A personality, much of my *feeling* of worth has come from what I do, who I'm with, and how many items are crossed off my "to-do" list by the end of the day. I'm not proud of that.

The lesson I'm still learning is that *I am valuable to God*. No flash. No media blitz. No big-time drama. No need to impress Him with my accomplishments, my associates, my looks, or my wardrobe. The plain and simple truth is that He finds me special!

With my personality, my sense of worth is at great risk when I accomplish far less than what my daily list requires, or when my schedule is drastically affected by unexpected interruptions or prolonged projects. Feelings of failure swoop in like birds of prey, leaving me feeling worthless and insignificant.

My expectation of being a "model Christian woman" has been disappointed again! I immediately long for a change. At the deepest level my longing is to have my disappointments filled with the satisfaction of God Himself. But emotions grip me. If I can pause at this point and think rationally about *who He is* and *who I am to Him,* my ruling passion will not be crazy workaholism (trying to "earn" His approval) or severe withdrawal ("I've failed before, and I'm a failure again, so I might as well quit trying.").

The bottom line is that God Himself finds me significant—so special, in fact, that He's given me the five crucial elements that authors Gary Smalley and John Trent identify in *The Blessing:*

• Meaningful touch

God touches my life every day through His Word, His creation, and other people. When a fellow believer puts an arm around me, sends a note of encouragement, or phones to say she's praying for me, I feel affirmed, special, and valued.

• A spoken message

Repeatedly in Scripture we are given a spoken message of love and affirmation. The Lord says in Jeremiah 31:3, "I have loved you with an everlasting love; I have drawn you with loving-kindness."

• Attaching "high value" to the one being blessed

What greater value could we ask for than to be created in the image of our heavenly Father? (Genesis 1:27).

• Picturing a special future for the one being blessed

Throughout the Bible, God reminds us of the unique, personally designed future He has already planned for us: "You have made known to me the path of life; you will fill me with joy in your presence, with eternal pleasures at your right hand" (Psalm 16:11).

• An active commitment to fulfill the blessing

The day we realize *we are not alone* is a very important day! Paul's words assure us of God's continuing involvement in fulfilling

His purpose through us: "Being confident of this, that he who began a good work in you will carry it on to completion until the day of Christ Jesus" (Philippians 1:6).[4]

POSTSCRIPT TO A NOBODY

In her book *God's Joyful Surprise,* Sue Monk Kidd beautifully states the depth of our longing: "The deepest need of the human heart is to be loved. To be loved utterly and completely just as we are, no matter what."[5]

Satan, the greatest deceiver of all time, knows that when our expectations of being special to someone are disappointed, we will long for change. If he can move quickly, we will be caught up in our emotions and make a bad decision based on ungodly beliefs. If he succeeds, our ruling passion will drive us to work to earn approval, practice inappropriate behavior in an attempt to gain attention, or withdraw.

But if we can evaluate our disappointments in time, we can choose a different course of action. By taking that deep longing for significance through the grid of our Christian convictions, our ruling passion will lead us to a decision that will glorify the God who created us.

It is God who loved us first. . . . He is the seeking Lover, the one who has made us for Himself. From the very beginning we were created to be found and loved by Him. He has woven this secret into the very fibers of our soul, and when we seek Him with all the longing He has planted in our hearts, in the end, we simply discover Him seeking us, loving us—in all times and all places.[6]

Our deepest passion for significance is finally satisfied when we realize He is all we need and we are "somebody" to Him.

CHAPTER 4

I Want to Do Something Worthwhile: To Have Meaningful Work

*It is not what a man does that determines
whether his work is sacred or secular, it is why
he does it. The motive is everything. Let a man
sanctify the Lord God in his heart and he can
thereafter do no common act.*

A. W. TOZER

"AND WHAT do *you* do for a living?" The sophisticated woman peered at me over her half-glasses and waited for a response. I stammered and broke eye contact while floundering for an image-building response.

For a moment I was speechless. Then, with a stutter, I blurted out, "I-I-I'm in education, but we moved recently, so I left my job as director of an alternative education program for pregnant teenagers, so I guess you'd say I'm a homemaker right now. I used to individualize coursework so pregnant teens could stay in school during their pregnancies. Part of my job involved coordinating the efforts of school social workers, health care professionals, and the parents of the girls. It was the most fulfilling work I've ever had."

My face flushed. I was embarrassed for having given such a lengthy description of my *former* position. I had never realized how much my self-esteem was locked into my professional status in the field of education. My husband had accepted a job that necessitated a move to another state, and for the first time in years I was without the significance connected with my former occupation.

I held the firm belief that *what* a person did for a living had nothing to do with her worth, intelligence, or value. But here I was, feeling like a nobody who had to apologize for joining the ranks of the "domestic engineers" by describing the details of my former "real" job.

My internal feedback was somewhat muddied, but I knew my response was a desperate attempt to be viewed as an important person by a woman I didn't even know. *"Good* Christian women shouldn't need titles, engraved brass plates on their front doors, or briefcases in their hands to know they are significant," I told myself. *"So why am I playing this game?"*

ANALYZING THE REACTION

When we meet someone for the first time, the question comes within minutes: "What do you do?" We're quick to assess a person's worth by our evaluation of the importance of their work. That leads us to the source of the disappointment of millions of women—even Christian women.

We have an expectation that we will have meaningful work that will provide a sense of worth. That expectation is often unfulfilled when our dreams of higher education are cut short, a baby interrupts our career, motherhood is not granted the "professional" status it deserves, we are trapped in a job beneath our aptitude or level of training, or good health is taken from us. Sometimes our disappointment comes with a gradual realization that day follows day and year follows year and we never seem to accomplish anything that seems important or significant.

As Christian women we have a deep longing to see God's purpose in our day-to-day activities. We *have a passion to know we are doing something worthwhile with our lives.*

THE SECULAR BELIEF SYSTEM

In a poll conducted for Robert Half International, a New York-based firm, the findings indicated that "one out of four Americans is unhappy in his or her job. The reasons? Workers most often mentioned their need for greater recognition, more money, less stress, and a better boss."[1]

In another study, "90 percent of U.S. high school students and 88 percent of their parents maintain that the primary purpose for a college education is to secure a job when you get out of school, make money, and eventually take it easy."[2]

As we listen to those in the media and talk with people on an everyday basis, there appear to be two reasons why the average person in twenty-first century America works outside the home.

First, to earn enough money to pay the bills and then to use the excess to enjoy life and accumulate "things." An old bumper sticker voices this philosophy: *He who dies with the most toys wins.* Many people view work as a "necessary evil" that is simply a means of attaining personal pleasure.

Second, to define "who I am." Many people are driven to succeed in their work in order to feel good about themselves. We somehow feel that what we *do* should describe what we *are.* This false philosophy is the trap I found myself in after leaving a fulfilling job when my husband was transferred.

Both Christian and nonChristian women struggle with the need to do something worthwhile. Some of us are driven by insecurity to become workaholics, only to find we're exhausted, unhappy, and struggling with feelings of failure. Too often we run our emotions through a distorted secular belief system.

How Does It Work?

Our Expectation: As Christian women we have a passionate desire to have a mission in life that validates our worth.

Our Disappointment: When we lose a meaningful job or become overwhelmed with the routine and sometimes frantic commitments of day-to-day living, we feel defeated.

If our mission is something we want and it has been taken away, we're disappointed. If, however, it's a mission that's been "thrust upon us," we may feel just as disappointed, wondering if the massive busyness is really accomplishing God's purpose.

Our Longing: Our disappointment leads to a desire for change. At the deepest level our desire is for a mission that fulfills God's agenda on earth. We long to know what our precise, customized task is that will validate our worth to Him and others.

Our Emotions: At this point the inner churning begins, and a variety of emotionally charged thoughts (and comments) emerge.

- "If I can't have that job, I'll never feel good about myself!"
- "I get so angry when I'm expected to do all this busywork; I never have time to do important things for God."

Our Belief System: With a basic knowledge of Scripture, our logic should lead us to a well-informed decision. Intellectually we know that God created us and loves us intensely. We know every activity in life has the potential of being used in an uncommon way for God's glory. As His ambassadors on this earth, we have a position of great significance as we faithfully live out our daily lives.

Our problem comes when we sift our emotions through the world's belief system. As we mull over the familiar question "What do *you* do for a living?" and as we view the status of those around us who have accumulated wealth, power, and prestige, we sometimes reach an ungodly decision.

Our Ruling Passion: If our values are securely rooted in the Word of God, we'll be convinced of our overwhelming worth to God regardless of our title, position, or "measurable" value. If, however, our convictions have been distorted by the way the secular world views "important people," we are likely to have a ruling passion that will lead us to depression or workaholism.

Our Action: The ruling passion will determine our action. I was very disappointed when my husband accepted the position that robbed me of a significant job. There was a major emotional struggle as I reviewed my situation, and lots of discussion with Gene about our options. But, ultimately, I knew my significance to God was not tied to my job with pregnant teens. With a belief system based on His Word, I was able to have a ruling passion that could result in an honorable action. In my case it was moving with my husband to a new location and believing I would be just as valuable to God without the benefit of my former position. (There were also special, unexpected benefits for me in this move that I had not anticipated.)

WHAT IS "MEANINGFUL" WORK?

Experts refer to work as "purposeful activity" that is revealed in three biblical dimensions: *expression*—that which expresses our abilities; *provision*—that which provides for our needs; and *mission*—that which accomplishes God's agenda on this earth.

As a Christian woman, I have spent the last several years of my life working in both secular employment and full-time Christian ministry. I am fully convinced that for the Christian there is no difference between the secular and the sacred with regard to the energy expended and the potential spiritual fruitfulness in both situations.

Working with women in Bible study and conference ministry for the past ten years has allowed me to counsel with enough individuals to learn that *all* women struggle with their self-worth when it comes to discovering their gifts and finding meaningful work. Most of us can point to at least one other woman who *appears* to have the perfect life situation that we secretly wish belonged to us.

For both married and single women, there are fabulous advantages and horrendous disadvantages to every life situation we could secretly desire, yet our sense of significance is intricately connected to our position and work in this world.

In the home in which I was raised, a high premium was placed on listening to God and then doing His will. During my junior high and high school years, my father made an indelible impression on me. After having run from God's call to the ministry for several years, Dad went back to Bible school and soon left the business world behind. With a wife and several children to support, it must have been a difficult decision. As I began my ninth-grade year, Dad took his first pastorate. Those were exciting days!

I watched Mom and Dad as they began to pour their lives into needy people. Mom's gift of hospitality and Dad's gift of evangelism worked like a hand in a glove to "love people into the kingdom of God."

"BURNING BUSH MENTALITY"

Going through my high school years during this high point in my parents' ministry meant that I was constantly exposed to Christianity at its most dramatic level. By the time I left home for my university years, I longed with every fiber of my being to make a difference in my world for Jesus Christ. The feeling must have been a lot like what Ray Ortlund, pastor of Lake Avenue Congregational Church in Pasadena, California, expressed in one of his books:

I had exclaimed in anguish many times in my life, "I refuse to be an ordinary Christian!"

I had pounded the pulpit and said, "I refuse to be an ordinary pastor! I refuse to pastor an ordinary church!"

Then I read a sentence from Thomas Kelly that set my heart on fire. He prayed, "Lord, make my life a miracle."

Oh, God! That's it! You're the original Miracle, and I live in You. Why shouldn't I be able to show others how to be miracles?[3]

I didn't yet know what God's plan was for my life, but one thing was certain—I was looking for my "burning bush" and I longed to hear Him tell me (preferably through a megaphone or on a neon sign) what He wanted me to do. He had worked dramatically in my parents' lives, and I expected the same. My significance would come from Him!

Promptly, I selected Psalm 16:11 (KJV) as my life verse: "Thou wilt show me the path of life: in thy presence is fulness of joy; at thy right hand there are pleasures for evermore." I was actively looking for my unique, personalized, immediate, and specific directions for following God's plan for my life. I was ready to set the world on fire!

MY SELFISH DEMAND

In Old Testament times, God often did the unusual to get the attention of people He was calling for important tasks. This was a day when the Holy Spirit did not reside within the hearts of men and women who believed in Him. There was no written Word of God in existence yet.

One of the Old Testament accounts that has always thrilled me is Exodus 3:2-5,9-10:

There the angel of the LORD appeared to him in flames of fire from within a bush. Moses saw that though the bush was on fire it did not burn up. So Moses thought, "I will go over and see this strange sight—why the bush does not burn up." . . . God called to him from within the bush, "Moses! Moses!"

And Moses said, "Here I am."

"Do not come any closer," God said. "Take off your sandals,

for the place where you are standing is holy ground. . . . The cry
of the Israelites has reached me, and I have seen the way the
Egyptians are oppressing them. So now, go. I am sending you to
Pharaoh to bring my people the Israelites out of Egypt."

I know I'm not the only person who would like to hear God's voice
in such a direct manner. The drama of the bush that could not be con-
sumed by fire, and God's voice speaking Moses' name from within has
always made me long for an emotionally charged calling for myself.

When I read this account in Scripture, I expect God to do something
big, flashy, and *personal* for me, too. I'm often looking for specific instruc-
tions for significant tasks, and when my mind is thus engaged I sometimes
miss God's most important voice to me through His Word. It can become
a subtle arrogance that cries, "Lord, if You don't show me Your will soon,
I'll know I'm not *really* important to You."

Such an attitude must grieve the heart of God. So often He is quietly at
work in powerful ways, revealing His will as I continue being faithful in the
daily affairs of life. Augustine wrote, "You were guiding me as a helmsman
steers a ship, but the course You steered was beyond my understanding."[4]

The fact is, God's purpose for our lives is already spelled out clearly
in Ephesians 1:11-14 (MSG):

It's in Christ that we find out who we are and what we are living
for. Long before we first heard of Christ and got our hopes up,
he had his eye on us, had designs on us for glorious living. . . .
It's in Christ that you, once you heard the truth and believed it
(this Message of your salvation), found yourselves home free—
signed, sealed, and delivered by the Holy Spirit. This signet from
God is the first installment on what's coming, a reminder that
we'll get everything God has planned for us, a praising and glorious life.

Our main goal in life is to live "a praising and glorious life." He has made the mystery of His will known to us and blessed us with the indwelling Holy Spirit.

On top of all that, He has uniquely gifted us for service. Read Romans 12:4-8, 1 Corinthians 12:27-31, and Ephesians 4:11-13. As we study these passages, we discover that there is no gender differentiation related to gifts given in the body of Christ. You and I are special to God, with significant gifts in the body of Christ. Without our contribution the body suffers.

I long to praise Him with the gifts, time, energy, and opportunities He has given to me during this lifetime. In his book *Desiring God,* John Piper stated,

> God's pursuit of praise from us and our pursuit of pleasure in
> him are one and the same pursuit. God's quest to be glorified
> and our quest to be satisfied reach their goal in this one experi-
> ence: our delight in God which overflows in praise.[5]

For me, living in fellowship with God and praising Him with my life involves working for Him. Work was meant to be a fulfilling experience. In fact, work was created *before* the fall of man, as we can see from Genesis 2:15: "The LORD God took the man and put him in the Garden of Eden to work it and take care of it." God knew that you and I needed meaningful work to be fulfilled human beings.

For many Christian women, parenting is a great work God gives them for a season of their lives. Ellen Wilson Fielding was book editor of the *Wall Street Journal,* married at age twenty-eight, and sometime later gave birth to a son. She encountered varied reactions from the people close to her when she announced she would be leaving her prestigious position to become an at-home mother. Her response? "I felt I was going to a greater thing when I left the *Wall Street Journal* to care for my son, because I was setting out to give more, more intensely, to a single human soul than I had been able to give for the millions of souls mildly affected by the book reviews I prepared for publication."[6]

Fielding's direction from the Lord may be different from His leading in your life or in my life; however, often the most fulfilling work we could have is the most obvious opportunity in our path today.

DEVELOPING A BIBLICAL BELIEF SYSTEM

It's clear that each of us is uniquely gifted for specific Christian service, whether we use our gifts in the secular or Christian arena. But where should we start when we have major questions about how God wants to use us? I believe there are at least five things we can do to discover the answers to those questions and make sure we are investing our lives in the things that are important to God.

SPEND TIME IN SOLITUDE EVERY DAY.

There's an old proverb that says, "Listen, or thy tongue will make thee deaf." My life can easily consist of waking up to the radio, the coffeepot, the shower, the daily stresses, the television, phone calls, and meal preparations, and if I have not pre-scheduled and *seized* a time to be alone with the Lord, there is none.

Sometimes my days are filled with the voices of other people—in person as well as through the media. I wonder if God sometimes tries to say, "Carol, I have something I'd like to tell you if I could get through the commotion so you could hear Me."

When you are alone with Him, make a special study of the God-given gifts mentioned in Scripture. (The passages were mentioned earlier in this chapter.) You will also find helpful guidance in the Bible study *Six Steps to Clarify Your Calling* (NavPress). As you study, pray, "Lord, what am I uniquely gifted to do in Your kingdom? How can You best be glorified in me?"

Discover How You're Wired.

For instance, you may have the specific spiritual gift of "helps" or "showing mercy," but you are really *wired* for a career in nursing. Other people may walk into a hospital, breathe the medicinal aroma, and feel ill themselves. You walk down the corridor of a health-care facility and your natural instinct is to *do something* for one of the patients.

You may attend a conference and immediately notice the lack of organization surrounding the scheduling, crowd control, and registration process. Your immediate reaction is to mentally lay out the way things *should have been done* to avoid confusion and problems. You have a God-given gift of "administration," and you are goal-oriented, efficient, and decisive. When you chair a committee, organize the church Christmas program, or function as a chief executive officer, everything runs smoothly and you feel good about it.

I'm *wired* for exhortation. When I'm with a group of believers and someone is struggling in a new position, I'm usually first to "come alongside" as a cheerleader and encourager. I've been training Christians in communication skills in "Speak Up With Confidence" seminars for the last few years, and almost nothing brings me more joy than seeing those with potential for sharing their faith or teaching the Word of God gain the confidence to speak up for Him!

I love to "drive home" specific truths from Scripture in such a way that people are motivated and deeply encouraged in their walks with God. My whole being wants to shout, "Hang in there! You can make it! Don't give up! You've just begun! I'm on your side!"

Listen to God's Voice.

In *Six Steps to Clarify Your Calling*, my coauthor, Karen Lee-Thorp, and I have itemized three facts that will assist you in embracing God's plan for your life.

1. God has a plan for my life that will maximize the use of my gifts for

His kingdom. David Frahm says, "God has made each of us His represen-tative steward, assigned to some tailored role in 'tending His garden.' We know that God has the whole world in His hands, certainly—but the question to ask is, What part of it has He assigned to *your* care?"[7]

2. God reveals His call on my life after I confess all sin in my heart, ver-balize my openness to His plan for my life, and make my life available for His direction. A wonderful way to express this response is through a prayer writ-ten by the authors of *Experiencing God:* "Lord, I will do anything that Your kingdom requires of me. Wherever You want me to be, I'll go. Whatever the circumstances, I'm willing to follow. If You want to meet a need through my life, I am Your servant; and I will do whatever is required."[8]

3. God's call on my life will be confirmed through His Word and through His Spirit. "The primary way God speaks to us is through His Word. Sometimes He speaks through the nudge of His Spirit, but we need to check those nudges against His Word—for His Spirit never leads against His Word."[9] Dee Brestin reminds us that God's tender call is always confirmed through Scripture.

I believe that God has gifted each of us in such a way that there are moments, while we are exercising our gift, that we have an inexplicable urge to shout, "Eureka!" That word is an interjection that indicates, "I found it!" It's a proclamation of surprise or pleasure upon finding that for which we've been looking.

Some time ago I was seated in a theater watching an exceptional film titled *Chariots of Fire*. This was the story of Eric Liddell, who later became a missionary to China until his death in the 1940s. As an Olympic athlete, Eric was in conflict regarding his giftedness and his personal convictions. He suddenly blurted out, "God made me so I run fast, and when I run I *feel* His pleasure."

I got a catch in my throat as he spoke. That's exactly how I feel when I teach people the Word of God and encourage people to be their best for the King of kings. God made me so I speak well. He designed me to be an encourager of other people, and when I use that gift I'm experiencing the joy of living in the smile of God's approval. Every believer can experience this. Each can discover her unique gift and present it to the Lord as a living sacrifice, "a praising and glorious life."

EXERCISE YOUR SPIRITUAL MUSCLE.

In prayer, dedicate yourself, your known gifts, your knowledge (however limited), and your *potential* to the Lord. Expose yourself to various tasks. Take advantage of opportunities to develop your gifts. Be actively pursuing God's highest calling for you!

LISTEN TO THE RESPONSES OF OTHERS.

There are two extremes that sadden my heart as I travel in ministry and hear the responses of women with regard to using God's gifts. One is the response of the woman who does not dare to believe God will do great things when He has opened every door for service, but instead continues to do nothing while saying, "Me? I couldn't do *that!*" The other is the one who lives in a fantasy world of constantly wishing to have gifts that seem more glamorous than the obvious gifts she possesses.

How do you know for sure that you have a gift? Consider the discernment of the people around you. What they say will give you clues. If you've wondered if you have a gift for teaching, try it. If people approach you afterward and say, "God really ministered to me through you today" or "I've never heard the gospel presented in such a clear and practical way before," that's a great affirmation that you have a gift for teaching.

On the other hand, if people fall asleep while you're talking and no one gives you the feedback that your message was a help to them, consider that God may want you to do more homework and try again or that perhaps your main gift is in an entirely different area. How wonderful it is to find out!

The story is told of a young boy who was auditioning for a part in the school play. His mother knew that he'd set his heart on receiving a part, though she was afraid he would not be chosen. On the day the parts were awarded, she drove to the school to pick him up. He rushed up to her, eyes shining with pride and excitement as he exclaimed, "Mom! Mom! I've been chosen to clap and cheer!"

Our importance to the body of Christ is discussed in 1 Corinthians 12:14-31 (MSG): "A body isn't a single part blown up into something huge. It's all the different-but-similar parts arranged and functioning together. . . . As it is, we see that God has carefully placed each part of the body right where he wanted it."

A PERSONAL CHALLENGE

I love to believe that God will do the impossible in the lives of ordinary people.

When Elisabeth Elliot was preparing to write *A Slow and Certain Light,* she read through the whole Bible to discover how God guided people. She states,

> I found that in the overwhelming majority of cases it was not
> through what we'd call "supernatural" means—voices, visions,
> angels, or miracles—but by natural means in the course of
> everyday circumstances when a man was simply doing what he
> was supposed to be doing (taking care of sheep or fighting a
> battle or mending fishnets).[10]

That's encouraging to me because most of my days are ordinary. I've wasted a lot of time jumping from here to there trying to find "God's perfect will" when He's already placed me in an obvious place to serve Him today. We are exhorted in Ecclesiastes 9:10: "Whatever your hand finds to do, do it with all your might." I long to recognize God's voice and to do His will. And I can—today—*if I choose to see all ground as holy ground.*

PART THREE:

The Passion for Security

CHAPTER 5

Why Me? Why This? Why Now?: To Accept Trials Gracefully

True atheists do not, I presume, feel disappointed in God. They expect nothing and receive nothing. But those who commit their lives to God, no matter what, instinctively expect something in return. Are those expectations wrong?

PHILIP YANCEY

THE COVER of the book intrigued me. A sticker on the front offered a money-back guarantee. *Clever marketing idea,* I thought. The book was the kind you hold with the title carefully concealed, so other people won't glance at it and automatically assume you have the problem stated in the title. But I *did* have the problem, and I *had* to buy that book! *Disappointment with God.*

I leafed through and read Philip Yancey's questions: *"Is God unfair? Why doesn't he consistently punish evil people and reward good people? Why do awful things happen to people good and bad, with no discernible pattern? . . . Is God silent? Is God hidden?"*[1]

My mind was racing. I hated those questions! It seemed blasphemous to think that God might be unfair, and it seemed heretical to admit that thought to someone else. As a preacher's kid, I'd memorized all the right answers. Romans 8:28 (KJV) was the "proper" response for all unexplainable grief: "And we know that all things work together for good to them that love God." I even had the manuscript of a talk I gave on suffering. It had three points—solid biblical points—that provided pat answers for the pain and hurts in the world. I hated that talk.

The day after I bought *Disappointment,* I declared a "day off" for myself. Dressed in jeans, I hurried through household chores so I could begin my reading. Within minutes I hated that book, too. Yancey asked questions without giving answers, and my personality type *demands* answers. I always buy "how-to" books that give ten solutions to a problem, with appropriate Scripture references listed with the correct answers. My basic philosophy has always been, "If you have a crisis, find out what caused it and fix it! If you look hard enough, pray intensely enough, and work long enough, you will discover the reason for your problem and there will be an obvious solution." Wrong!

DISAPPOINTMENT WITH GOD?

Draping my legs over an arm of my most comfortable chair, I "settled in." The feather cushion accepted the strange contours of my improper posture and formed a comfortable theater seat for the mental cinema that was about to begin. The deeply felt vignette would be from my life—a disappointment that I blamed God for (subliminally, of course, because I had never been able to admit that I was angry at Him).

My Expectation: Our son, J. P., was five years old, and Gene and I were thinking seriously about having another baby. We were comfortable in our spacious suburban home and felt God had blessed us with the love and resources to share with another child.

To our surprise, the miracle of conception occurred sooner than we had anticipated. We weren't the youngest parents-to-be in our circle of friends, so we knew our "little secret" would be quite a surprise. We decided to wait a while to announce the good news.

My Disappointment: One day as always, I was running at breakneck speed—kindergarten car pool for J. P., Bible Study Fellowship classes to teach, household responsibilities to tend to, correspondence to answer, and speeches to prepare. I had experienced some cramping during the early weeks of pregnancy and tried to slow my pace a bit. "It's normal," I told myself. "It's been so long since my last pregnancy. I just don't remember all these uncomfortable aches and pains that come with an expanding uterus." In spite of my rationalization, I had a nagging thought that the cramps were *not* normal.

The next day I left home early for a speaking engagement on the Canadian side of the border. Waiting to go through customs, I again felt painful abdominal tightening. Two hours into the trip, the cramps felt more like vise grips. Something was wrong. "Lord," I prayed, "please take care of this baby. I don't know what to do."

I was alone in a rural area in a foreign country, headed for a town with no hospital. The practical side of me took over and I gave myself a pep talk. "You've been having cramps regularly; this is no cause for alarm. You can stand this pain and make it through this speaking engagement. Over two hundred people are expecting you momentarily, and you can't let them down."

Arriving at my destination, I found myself in a community center and went immediately to the restroom. Graffiti covered the walls and filthy debris was scattered here and there on the floor. The smell indicated a desperate need for a plumber (or at least a custodian). My brief walk from the car was accompanied by severe abdominal pains, and sitting in that vulgar stall, I knew I was losing my baby. Within five minutes it was over. I was no longer pregnant.

The instant waves of depression were much worse than the physical discomfort, but I buried my emotions and went in to speak to those women.

My Longing: The meeting had already begun. After the introduction, I walked to the lectern. There, three rows back, directly in front of me, sat a woman with her darling infant in her arms. For an instant I didn't remember why I was there. She had a baby and I wanted one. The woman was holding what my heart longed for. I wanted my baby back in my womb, not flushed down a filthy toilet in a run-down community building!

My Emotions: I wanted to scream. It was so unfair. *God was so unfair!* Emotions pulsed through my heart and my breathing was irregular. My wild thoughts were directed heavenward. *Why? Why did You allow this to happen? I'm traveling alone. I am a good mother. I wanted that baby. Here I am serving You, working for You, investing my time in "eternal stuff," and You— God of the universe, Worker of miracles, mighty Healer— allowed me to lose this baby in that perverse, stinking washroom! Then, like rubbing salt in my wound, You allow that breast-feeding mother to sit in the third row! Yes, You are unfair!*

My Belief System: It was time to begin. The pause before my opening remarks had already been too long. My internal furor, totally directed toward God, seemed foreign. With precise timing, guilt suddenly swept through me, temporarily knocking anger aside. My past years of Christian training provided a belief system that I didn't instantly recognize as flawed. I told myself, *Mature Christians know God is in control during every crisis, even though they can't see Him at work. Forget your pain and do the right thing— give the speech and try not to look at the baby in the third row.*

My Ruling Passion: If my values had been properly established on biblical truth, if I had been convinced of my security in God as my Abba Father (my own dear Daddy), my ruling passion could have been acceptance of my pain and hurt, including the accompanying grief. Instead, my ruling passion was denial.

My Actions: That day, I carried on with my responsibilities like a programmed Christian robot. The speech I gave to that group was presented as if someone had plugged in a DVD. It had predictable content and an evangelistic ending. I didn't admit my personal devastation to anyone in the group. On the way home I allowed myself the brief luxury of sobbing without embarrassment. My baby was gone! Then, almost as if on cue, I began my action of denial (which I truly believed was godly).

I minimized the physical pain and exhaustion I was feeling from the miscarriage. I pushed down the deep emotional agony of the loss and made light of the whole event with the handful of friends who knew about the pregnancy. By internally denying myself "mourning time" and instantly carrying on with major responsibilities, I was sure God would be more pleased with me.

THE PASSION FOR SECURITY

We have an insatiable desire for security! When we're secure, we feel safe and removed from danger. We experience freedom from doubt. There are three major places where we look for security, and when our expectations are unfulfilled in those areas, we experience disappointment.

POSSESSIONS

As Christian women, we know *real* security does not lie in what we possess, but often we're more attached to "things" than we might admit. Several farmers in our area have been in deep financial difficulty due to drought and low market prices. One day my friend said, "Carol, when I became a farmer's wife I never considered that there would be a day I'd have to give up my home. We are going bankrupt. I've been upset, but my emotions went through the roof the day we had to sell my grandmother's china and silverware in an auction in order to liquidate our assets. Those items were heirlooms that would have been passed on to my children. I feel so guilty for crying about such a little thing. Before that auction I never knew how attached I was to 'things.'" *Disappointment!*

CIRCUMSTANCES

It's easy to forget how often our security is tied to favorable circumstances. When events in our lives flow smoothly, life seems good. But when dramatic circumstances change the course of our lives, it's another story. A teenaged son is hit by a drunk driver and left with paralysis; a baby is born with Down's syndrome; a daughter gets hooked on drugs; a friend is raped and later discovers she is pregnant; a good job is lost; unexpected health problems occur. Suddenly, often without warning, we struggle with deep insecurities. *Disappointment!*

PEOPLE

Relationships are the cause of our deepest joys and our most complex trials. We feel like our heart is breaking in two when a husband leaves us, or our reputation is ruined by a coworker, or our best friend turns on us. The experiences of birth and death can also be traumatic "shakers-of-security." In most cases, the deeper our experience of intimacy with another person, the greater the chance for hurt as a result of a misunderstanding, personal attack, or withdrawal. As Reuben Welch wrote, "We really do *need* each other!" And when our personal relationships are threatened, our security blanket is torn out of our hands. *Disappointment!*

Few things cause us the kind of surging emotion that a loss of security does, whether that comes through unexplainable trials or life's major change points.

DIFFICULT QUESTIONS

It's hard to believe in the goodness of God when personal disaster strikes. Every day tragedies occur all around us. Our hearts want to scream, "Why, Lord? Where are You, God, when these horrible things happen? Do You care?"

One of our deep emotions of the heart is anger—even anger directed toward God—when we go through life's trials. There's something in us that fights back and cries out, "It's not fair! I don't deserve this! Obviously God doesn't love me!" Then, as Christians, we feel guilty for having those thoughts.

THE GUILT SYNDROME

I have so much experience with guilt that I could start a franchise. I can see the neon sign now: "GUILT, INC., Founder and Director, Carol Kent. (Franchises available in your city with no money down.)" The promotional material could advertise my credentials:

Carol automatically feels guilty about everything she should have done or could have done better. She's a born people-pleaser. If you are unhappy with her performance, she knows she's wrong, not you. She feels insecure if anyone in her sphere of influence sees her as spiritually weak, and she feels responsible to automatically reflect the truth she teaches regarding biblical principles. She feels especially guilty for occasionally doubting God and for having negative thoughts about His fairness. If her feelings of insecurity might be a bad example to someone else, she will fake what her Christian programming says is the proper response. Her programming has been so complete that it's often an automatic response that takes no thought at all. Frequently she feels like it's the "spiritual" thing to do.

Many of us who are active members of this exclusive "guilt-trip" club have developed a flawed belief system. Some of the myths we have come to believe are the following:

- I must be a perfect Christian.
- Everyone should love me and approve of me.
- If I am a good Christian, life should be fair.
- It's a sin to feel depressed.
- If I am living in fellowship with God, I should never feel anger toward Him or other people.
- It's my job to meet everyone's needs.
- If I feel worried, I'm a bad Christian.
- If God loved me, bad things would not happen to me.
- God will bless me with health and happiness if I work hard for Him.
- When there is so much *real* tragedy in the world, it's wrong for me to feel grief over little things.

As the firstborn of six children, leadership was a "natural" for me. Coming to know Christ at a young age and being raised in the church gave me a wonderful background in biblical truths and key Scriptures. It wasn't until I evaluated my response following the loss of my baby that I began to admit how distorted my belief system had become.

I had expected a healthy baby that would fill our lives with more joy than we could imagine. Disappointment was keen on the day of the miscarriage. The dirty community center and the newborn in the audience intensified my disappointment with God. I longed to pretend my loss was a dream and I'd wake to find that my miracle-working God had restored my pregnancy. Everything in my background taught me that God was fair. He was just. I knew nothing could touch me without His permission. Somehow that thought made me feel the miscarriage was His fault. As my decision-making process ran through my belief system, which was a combination of truth and the myths I've just listed, my ruling passion became denial. With my destructive thought process, my denial wound up driving me to several actions.

First, I didn't admit that I was physically weak and emotionally and spiritually devastated by the miscarriage.

Second, I lied to people by acting as if the loss was "no big deal . . . the baby was only in the embryo stage anyway . . . it wasn't like a still-birth." (The lie wasn't consciously spoken; it was part of the conditioned response I thought a good Christian should give.)

Third, I experienced a "slow simmer" that gradually became a bubbling caldron of anger toward God for taking my baby and adding to my pain with so many negative happenings on the day of the miscarriage. The initial anger would not have become sin if I'd had a God-honoring ruling passion (to be transparent and honest with Him, committed to working *through* my feelings rather than allowing my anger to grow by pretending it wasn't there).

Fourth, over the next few years, creeping bitterness established a major root system within me. Occasionally someone would say, "I see you have only one child; I assume you're so busy in your career you really don't have time for the responsibility of another baby." (I felt like I'd been stabbed with a knife.)

One day a woman visited in my home and said, "I'd have nice furniture, too, if I'd chosen to have only one child and had gone to work." (Her unspoken accusation regarding my "materialistic" reason for being the mother of one made my blood boil!)

If my belief system had been based on true Christian principles, it would have included permission to experience deep grief; it would have freed me to acknowledge my physical condition the day I lost the baby. The Christian women's luncheon would not have been ruined if I had been unable to speak—even at the last minute. My belief system should have included a clause that read: "She does not have to be a superwoman when life falls apart. She can cry when she hurts, and God will still love her if she acknowledges 'negative' emotions." With a ruling passion of denial, I didn't accept responsibility for sinful bitterness that affected my relationships with other people and with God over a period of years.

THE GUILT INTENSIFIES

I feel insecure when I'm not in control. That's a scary thing to admit. My disappointment with God does not come only in the major trials of life; it also comes with the small stuff. One bitterly cold Saturday night in February, I was driving home from a conference. In pitch darkness on a very busy highway, my car suddenly lost all of its electrical power—no lights, no heat, no power steering!

Two hours later my hands were numb with cold, a mechanic I didn't know had total authority over my car (and my pocketbook), and I was told that it would be at least twenty-four hours before the "missing belt" on my vehicle could be replaced. Sitting in a motel in a strange city, I knew I would miss a scheduled meeting the next day and I would be liable for whatever the mechanic decided to charge. I felt like a victim, and I was angry at God.

Did God care about my tremendous frustration and my loss of time, money, and emotional energy? My disappointment brought a longing for change (a car that ran well, accompanied by no interruptions or financial distress). After expressing my negative emotions, first to the desk clerk and then to God, I felt guilty! Another myth came rushing in: *When there is so much real tragedy in the world, it's wrong for me to feel grief over little things.* Wrong again!

KILLING THE MYTHS AND BUILDING SOUND VALUES

I'm writing this book for people like me who want to learn the secret of handling disappointments in the right way, so the passions that rule us will be powerful forces for good rather than evil. If we are living by an internal list of myths that we believe are "spiritual," when indeed they are not, we will wind up with destructive, misguided ruling passions.

Once I faced the denial of the pain of my miscarriage, it was like someone lifted a veil off my understanding. Finally I could point to one incident after another in my life in which I had sacrificed an honorable or a holy passion because I was living under a flawed belief system. I reviewed my list of myths again:

- I must be a perfect Christian.
- Everyone should love me and approve of me.
- If I am a good Christian, life should be fair.
- It's a sin to feel depressed.
- If I am living in fellowship with God, I should never feel anger toward Him or other people.
- It's my job to meet everyone's needs.
- If I feel worried, I'm a bad Christian.
- If God loved me, bad things would not happen to me.
- God will bless me with health and happiness if I work hard for Him.
- When there is so much *real* tragedy in the world, it's wrong for me to feel grief over little things.

It was painful to admit that these "convictions" were not based on truth. I had based so many of my responses to trials in my life on flawed thinking, and my ruling passions resulted in actions that did not please God.

Replacing our myths with truth develops convictions that result in godly ruling passions. Instead of experiencing guilt for feeling and expressing our negative emotions and thus denying our pain, we can admit the struggle involved in the Christian life. It is not a sin to struggle. The apostle Peter said, "Friends, when life gets really difficult, don't jump to the conclusion that God isn't on the job" (1 Peter 4:12, MSG).

Bible teacher and conference speaker Dr. Stephen Olford once had a college student approach him with a question. The young man had his notebook and pen in hand and asked, "Tell me, what are the keys to Christian leadership?"

I'm sure this fellow was all set to write down ten easy steps to Christian maturity. Dr. Olford began, "The keys to Christian leadership are *bent knees, wet eyes,* and *a broken heart.*"[2] Psalm 51:17 (MSG) says, "I learned God-worship when my pride was shattered. Heart-shattered lives ready for love don't for a moment escape God's notice."

I sometimes forget that God designed me to live in a perfect world, but because of sin I live in a "groaning" world—filled with imperfect people, flawed values, disease, crime, war, unexplainable circumstances, and irritating Christians. My security is threatened when people let me down and when I let myself down again and again! If I believe my "myths," my ruling passions will be destructive.

Job reminds us that life is unfair and that being faithful to God does not mean our lives will automatically be filled with good health and happiness. Job's family died, his possessions were taken away, all circumstances that could turn on him did, his best friends thought he was a fool, and his wife told him to "curse God and die!"

In the middle of Job's trials, we feel his emotional response to his disappointments: "I shout for help, God, and get nothing, no answer! . . . I expected good but evil showed up. I looked for light but darkness fell. My stomach's in a constant churning, never settles down. Each day confronts me with more suffering" (Job 30:20,26-27, MSG).

Healthy beliefs allow us to recognize a disappointment, understand the longing it produces, *feel and express the pain of the emotional rush,* and run the decision-making process through truth—not myth—in order to choose a ruling passion that will glorify God as it becomes an action. David said in Psalm 56:8 (MSG), "You've kept track of my every toss and turn through the sleepless nights, Each tear entered in your ledger, each ache written in your book."

A week after I spoke for a retreat, a letter arrived from one of the participants. She had never attended a Christian women's conference before and said she only came with her friend, Connie, because she wanted some time away and "the price was right." She wrote,

Dear Carol,

. . . after the first meeting, Connie and I knew we were meant to
be there. We talked late on Friday night and all Saturday afternoon and I finally shared something I had determined I would
never tell another soul. Even after the tears and comforting from
Connie I could not pray—all I could feel was tremendous
anger—and then the question—why? I was only eight years
old. I didn't deserve it, and yet I have felt such tremendous guilt
all these years!

When you started speaking and told about the sixteen-year-
old who had trusted a man for a ride and how he raped her, my
tears started again as my own memories of the past flashed
before me.

When you asked if we knew that "bad things happen to
good Christian people," the walls completely crumbled, and by
the end of your talk I knew why I could not communicate with
the Lord. I had completely closed communication with Him
because I was so furious! I could not believe that He would
have let that awful thing happen to me if He truly loved me. I
had built my whole Christian life on a false set of ideals, forgetting that we live in a world that is fallen and full of hurts.

Feeding my emotions into faulty convictions, I believed that
God was unfair, cruel, and hidden. My ruling passion, although I
didn't consciously recognize it, was anger that was acted out by
withdrawing from God and Christianity and building a wall
between me and any human being who might hurt me. I'm just
coming to grips with the fact that God does love me very much.

You encouraged me when you said that God could take
any negative in our lives and turn it into a *positive.*

I'm thirty-nine years old and this is the first time I have genuinely experienced God's love, accepted what happened in my life, and expressed and released my anger. I have a long way to go, but this weekend was a new beginning for me.

CHANGING OUR THINKING TAKES TIME

I'm still reprogramming my mind with truth. I try to study biblical passages that replace my "myths" with statements that are based on fact. Insensitive comments about my "only" child don't hurt as much as they used to—but I can now admit that they *do* hurt! For me, that's a big step toward a more healthy values system. God doesn't expect me to be superhuman.

Memorizing Scripture has been a big help, but it's harder to memorize than it used to be and it's tough to climb out of old ruts, even if they're uncomfortable. Being honest about my emotions when I'm disappointed with God is still my most difficult hurdle, but I'm making progress. Philip Yancey's insights are a good reminder:

> The Spirit will not remove all disappointment with God. The very titles given to the Spirit—Intercessor, Helper, Counselor, Comforter—imply there will be problems. But the Spirit is also "a deposit, guaranteeing what is to come," Paul said, drawing on an earthly metaphor from the financial world. The Spirit reminds us that such disappointments are temporary, a prelude to an eternal life with God. God deemed it necessary to restore the spiritual link *before* re-creating heaven and earth.[3]

Right now life is hard and life is unfair. Larry Crabb reminds us that, while we live in this fallen world, we will groan or pretend we don't![4] But my hope is firm and I have great security that there's a better day coming!

CHAPTER 6

Lord, Make Me Flexible!:
To Adapt to Change Joyfully

*If your security is based on something that can
be taken away from you— you will constantly
be on a false edge of security.*
TIM HANSEL

MY HEART sank as I opened a letter and read this note from my
friend Linda:

Carol, my entire life has changed in a matter of a few weeks.
My mother has been diagnosed with Alzheimer's disease and
can no longer care for herself. She has moved into our home
and totally disrupted my whole world. I was so looking forward
to being with you for the "Speak Up With Confidence" seminar,
but I'll need to cancel my registration and ask for your prayer.
I'm discovering that my mother has become my child and I have
become her parent. On some days I handle the situation with
dignity; at other times I scream and hit the walls.

My husband has informed me that he cannot cope with my

mother by himself, even for a short time. He is angry with the way she is interfering with every aspect of our lives. We are fighting constantly and no longer have any privacy.

This has been the most difficult change point in my life. I love my mother deeply, but at times I can't stand to be in the same room with her. She asks the same questions repeatedly and there are days when I think I'm going crazy. We can't afford full-time nursing care for her, and the future looks hopeless.

A month earlier Linda had mailed her registration with the attached note: "I've been waiting for this seminar for three years—and I can hardly wait to be there! God continues to open doors for me to speak, and I need more training." Then suddenly, without warning, her whole life was turned upside down by the health crisis of her mother. All of her personal plans had to be put on hold.

One of my deep longings is to be strong enough as a Christian woman to adapt to change joyfully, no matter what! For years I've quoted from such Scriptures as, "But those who hope in the LORD will renew their strength. They will soar on wings like eagles; they will run and not grow weary, they will walk and not be faint" (Isaiah 40:31). But I wonder if I'd be "soaring like an eagle" if Linda's situation were mine. I doubt it.

UNDERSTANDING CHANGE

I think of change as "anything that rocks my boat." And change has great potential for threatening our sense of security. Some changes are of major importance and determine how the next several years of our lives will be lived. Other changes are much less life-altering. Occasionally changes bring excitement, but even when they're positive there's always some degree of stress involved.

The experts tell us that traumas, transitions, and changes occur throughout our lives and can usually be divided into the following three groups.

ANTICIPATED CHANGES

This category involves major life events that many of us expect to be part of our lives, such as entering the workforce or getting married or having a child.

UNEXPECTED CHANGES

These changes can disrupt our lives completely because they cannot always be anticipated. They may include such things as emergency surgery, the loss of a job, or an accident that leaves us or someone we love disabled. It could also mean something as devastating as a divorce or as exhilarating as receiving an inheritance. Unexpected change often disrupts our lives so completely that we are *never* the same again.

NO CHANGES

This category involves events we believed would happen, but they didn't. Perhaps we always wanted to own a home but we've never been able to afford one. It could be that we thought we'd eventually marry, but we never met the right person. We might long for a baby but discover we are infertile. There was never a particular day when we knew these hopes wouldn't be fulfilled, but slowly the realization dawned.

CHANGES AFFECT OUR SENSE OF SECURITY

I've been a failure when it comes to adapting to change joyfully. Even positive changes bring stress to our lives. And changes we perceive as negative can rip our heart out, destroy our confidence, and leave us emotionally vulnerable.

In these two chapters, we're talking about the passion for security. So much of my sense of safety and stability comes from the feeling (real or imagined) of being protected, certain of my current conditions, and free from doubt or worries. When changes occur and my "safe" situation is altered, I come face-to-face with disappointments. Longings are born and emotions take over. I now have a choice. Will I decide on a ruling passion that will result in an honorable or holy action, or will I be influenced by faulty values and choose an inappropriate response?

In the last chapter, we talked about the trials that come from our loss of security in the areas of *possessions* and unexpected *circumstances*. In this chapter, we're focusing on change and how it affects *relationships*.

LINDA'S CHANGE—UNEXPECTED AND UNWANTED

A closer look at Linda's responses when her ill mother moved in may help us to understand ourselves.

Linda's Expectation: She believed life would be easy, with relatively few stresses, as long as she was living close to the Lord.

Linda's Disappointment: Her mother's health crisis brought several unwanted changes:

- A live-in "houseguest" who needed constant attention
- Tremendous stress in her marriage and in her family relationships
- A massive interruption in her personal plans for training and ministry opportunities

Linda's Longing: Her entire being longed for life as it used to be— normal!

Linda's Emotions: Linda's emotions were volatile. She loved her mother, feeling deep compassion for her one minute and yet almost hating her the next. She was irritated with her husband for "distancing" himself from the problem, but then she'd become angry when he offered too much advice. Linda's emotions gave way to feelings of despair when she realized her life and her plans were suddenly—and indefinitely—"on hold."

Linda's Belief System: Linda's belief system had appeared moderately healthy under stress-free conditions, but it contained holes that soon surfaced. Her "myths" negatively affected her ruling passion:

- It's my job to handle every crisis myself.
- I should give up all my personal plans to meet the needs of everyone else.
- I can't be happy if life is harder than I expected.

Linda's Ruling Passion: Since Linda's decision-making process was sifted through this damaged set of convictions instead of biblically sound values, her ruling passion was depression.

Linda's Actions: Her actions involved a series of choices that were misguided:

- Continuous conflict with her husband
- Begrudging care of her mother rather than loving service
- Withdrawal from all church and ministry involvement, accompanied by a defeatist attitude

Fortunately it's never too late to evaluate our longings and resulting emotions in the light of God's Word. Linda's deep love for the Lord and her husband, mother, and sister soon drove her to carefully study her initial responses. With the help of a Christian counselor, she was able to change her thinking and "rewrite" her convictions. Positive change didn't happen overnight, but she finally realized three important things:

- She does *not* have to handle every crisis herself. (She has a myriad of friends and family who are willing to help if she will give up her controlling attitude.)

- Being godly does *not* mean giving up all personal plans and resorting to the life of a hermit. Finances may be tight, but there are social agencies, nonprofit organizations, and support groups in her city that can offer assistance.
- She can be joy-filled, even if life is harder than she expected. This is tough, especially on her mother's "bad" days and on her own hormonal "down" periods. These times demand a sense of humor, flexibility, time alone with God, frequent mini-getaways with her husband, nurturing friendships, and an eternal viewpoint.

With these changes in place, her ruling passion has been acceptance, not resignation, and her resulting actions have reflected honorable choices that have brought glory to God and a positive challenge to observers.

EMOTIONAL TRIGGER POINTS

Often the first *recognizable* problem I have with change is an emotional reaction. Most of the time I haven't thought about the disappointment that created the longing that, in turn, prompted my reaction. That's danger-ous—because then I automatically "read into" the situation and convince myself that *it's not my problem!* If someone else were a more perfect per-son or if these negative events hadn't transpired, then I would not be in an emotional upheaval. I then subtly blame other people for my resulting action without ever taking responsibility for my own ruling passion.

There are many emotional trigger points prompted by changes in our lives that can drastically affect our relationships. Some changes have great potential for "rocking our boat."

CHANGE OF NEIGHBORS

My doorbell rang. I casually opened the door while picking the remains of an Oreo cookie out of my front teeth. There stood an attractive man with his hand outstretched, saying, "Hello, Mrs. Kent, I'm going to be your new neighbor. I'm stopping by to tell you that we will be putting up a fence this weekend along the line that connects our backyard with yours. We raise German shepherds, and we'll be constructing a dog run. I certainly hope that won't be a problem to you."

I smiled and stuck out my hand. "Welcome to the neighborhood." My emotions were going crazy. While making polite conversation on the outside, I was screaming on the inside. My office window faces that property line! My bedroom faces that property line! My informal dining area and back deck both face that property line! A fence will destroy the beauty of the wooded area between our houses. I cannot work on my manuscripts, have meaningful devotions, get a good night's sleep, and entertain company for a barbecue on my deck with a chorus of dogs barking! And what about my property value?

My comfortable little boat was being rocked. My expectation of peaceful life in the suburbs was being destroyed, and I longed for the continuation of life as it was—before the new neighbors! As this emotional stream of thoughts settled a bit, I realized I was jumping to conclusions and the action resulting from my ruling passion in this matter could determine the new neighbor's eventual response to my Christianity.

The "ripple" effect on relationships, initiated by something as "small" as this change in neighbors, could eventually involve:

- Stress between me and my husband, because he would probably not complain about the situation unless it became unbearable.
- A subtle "silent treatment" between me and the neighbors who "stole" my serene lifestyle.
- A wall between me and God because of my negative attitude. Couldn't He have kept it from happening?

Our initial emotional reactions are *not* sin. When we sift the emotions through our convictions, *we choose our own ruling passion* and the actions that follow. In the relationship struggles previously mentioned, the potential negative actions will all be a result of my own ruling passion. That's where sin enters the picture.

CHANGE OF PLANS

This type of change occurs almost daily and can be disappointing, but it usually doesn't cause a major upheaval in our lives. It might be a canceled appointment or a postponed visit with a friend or relative. Occasionally it's unexpected company.

CHANGE IN HOUSING

A move, even a *desired* move, brings tremendous stress to most women. There is mental exhaustion regarding *where* to move, *what* to move into (house, condo, apartment), and *how* to take care of financing. Then comes the work of packing as well as determining what to keep, what to give away, and what to throw away. If you are single and have to take full responsibility for all decisions, moving can be even more emotionally taxing.

CHANGE IN EMPLOYMENT

With more women working outside the home than ever before, a majority of us are going through numerous changes in regard to job placement and relationships as the heavy stresses of divided domestic labor and child-care responsibilities are worked out.

CHANGE IN MARITAL STATUS

Going from single living to being married can be a shocking experience. Even if the changes that accompany marriage were desired, there are major conflicts when two people begin living under one roof! Soon "character flaws" and various tensions become evident.

All of us who've experienced marriage can identify with the story of young Susie. Her elementary school teacher observed her playing a game called "Wedding" during recess. Explaining the game to her teacher, she said, "I'm the bride, Sarah is the bridesmaid, and Jennifer is the flower girl."

The teacher looked puzzled and asked, "Well, then, who's the groom?"

"Oh, teacher, we don't need a groom. I only want a small wedding."

On some days the thought *has* occurred to me that marriage would be a whole lot easier without the groom! Our disappointments often create longings for a more perfect spouse.

A traumatic change usually occurs when a marriage ends—either through death or divorce. On the average, women live about seven years longer than men, so many of us will face the major change of going from marriage to widowhood. The divorce rate in the United States remains close to the 50 percent mark, so half of all married women will become acquainted with the difficult changes that occur when a marriage ends.

CHANGE IN FAMILY ROLE

There is almost nothing that changes a household more than the arrival of a baby! Suddenly this little twenty-inch-long human being, weighing less than ten pounds, takes over and expects you to jump every time he cries. Life will never be the same again! We run to them when they cry, and we wonder what they are doing when they are too quiet. Someone wisely said, "Children are like mosquitoes—the moment they stop making noises you know they're getting into something." Yes, motherhood *does* change life considerably!

Many women become "instant mothers" of extra children when families are blended. For some of these moms, it's a tremendously difficult challenge to bring two families together, especially if the children from both families are to live under the same roof. The mother comes into the marriage with an expectation that her biological children will have a full-time father and that they'll be a complete and loving family—but often there are agonizing disappointments.

CHANGE IN AGE

Each season of life brings new potential for living out our dreams and new opportunities for experiencing disappointments. With our youth comes a tremendous sense of optimism and hope. As the years go by, major decisions are made—to marry or to remain single, to take a job or to stay at home. When menopause comes and our biological time clock runs out, there is a special sense of the passing of time and the shortness of life.

CHANGE IN RESPONSIBILITIES

Sharon and I had lunch one day, and she said, "For the last two years I've been the chairwoman for a Christian women's organization, and I've complained daily about the hours of work I've been doing on a voluntary basis. Finally someone else accepted this position and removed the workload from my shoulders. Even though it was my choice to be replaced all along, I'm missing my former responsibilities. With this sudden change I'm experiencing a sense of loss."

CHANGE IN HEALTH—A PERSONAL CRISIS

Most of us can cope with daily problems as long as we are physically healthy, but when we are coping with an illness or a disability, even small incidents seem like major mountains.

I have been grateful for excellent health and a high energy level for most of my life. It used to be difficult for me to empathize with people who endure chronic pain. Then it happened. A few years ago I grabbed a heavy suitcase out of the trunk when I was running to catch a plane. Searing pain tore through my back, letting me know that something major had gone wrong.

For months, on a daily basis, I woke up in excruciating pain. After a few hours of torturous movement each morning, the pain level was reduced enough to allow me to carry on with most of my activities. The problem was diagnosed as a herniated disc. There was medication that proved somewhat helpful, but for the most part severe pain lasted for a period of several months.

My Expectation: My subliminal expectation was for perfect health for my entire lifetime. I never consciously considered it an expectation, because I always took good health and a high energy level for granted.

My Disappointment: I had committed myself to an arduous schedule of retreat and conference engagements. Costly publicity materials were already printed and distributed for several seminars. I was determined to fulfill my obligations and assumed that God would take away the pain. But I was sadly disappointed.

My Longing: I simply longed to get up in the morning free of the "fireball" in my lower back and function like a normal human being.

My Emotions: My initial reaction was predictable: "Deny this pain and it will go away. If you work hard, it will take your mind off the pinched nerve and you will be able to carry on with life." But pain has its own mind, and day after day there were moments when hope was eroded by despair.

Emotions built up within me. Sitting in the office of an orthopedic surgeon, I begged, "Please give me a prescription that will kill this pain without making me drowsy. I do not have time for this ridiculous inconvenience!" The doctor let me know my problem had no "instant" cures, nor could he promise the pain would go away. He suggested bed rest. I was furious!

Standing in the shower the next morning, I leaned forward to wash my foot, only to discover I was physically incapable of bending that far without crying out in physical anguish. I was hurting, and I was mad at God. Through my tears I screamed, "It isn't fair! I can't believe You are allowing me to suffer like this!" I felt humiliated when I had to have assistance with tasks as routine as getting dressed.

My Belief System: I knew from my upbringing that God's goal is for each of us to be conformed to the image of Christ (see Romans 8:29), and

I knew, intellectually, that pain was part of the process for the Lord Jesus and often is for us, too. Practical application of that truth was harder to make as I found myself in the grip of inflammation and pain that extended from my left hip to my ankle. Slowly, pain chipped away at my convictions, and I meditated on myths that were buried in my subconscious Christian mindset:

- I cannot be joyful if I'm not in control.
- If God really loved me, He would rid me of this pain.
- I must not tell anyone that I doubt the justice of God, because that would be a bad testimony.

My Ruling Passion: I chose a ruling passion based on the faulty beliefs expressed in those myths. I decided to "tough it out for Jesus" for all of the wrong reasons.

My Action: This health change in my life caused a severe disappointment that fueled the longing for a body free of pain. When that didn't happen right away and I based my ruling passion on faulty convictions, my actions were misguided and displeasing to God.

My change in health drastically affected my relationships with other people. On the surface, to people close to me, it appeared that pain altered my mood, my tolerance of others, my ability to work, my sense of security, my feelings of self-worth, and at times, my relationship with God. But in each individual situation, I made choices based on my negative ruling passion. To people outside the inner circle, I appeared energetic, in control, joyful, and spiritual, with very few people guessing my physical agony. But my specific actions reflected my flawed values:

- I quit reading the Bible and found it impossible to pray.
- I went through the motions of ministry while simultaneously doubting God and feeling anger toward Him. This dichotomy in

my spiritual life caused guilt and a subtle, growing depression.

- I became emotionally attached to a physician who understood my severe pain and had genuine compassion for my physical need. There was no immoral behavior or even inappropriate conduct between us, but my heart knew the potential was there because of my disappointment with God, fueled by intellectual chemistry and physical need for the regular doctor's appointments.

POSITIVE CHANGE IN OUR THINKING IS POSSIBLE

Fortunately, it's never too late to evaluate a flawed set of values and rewrite them with sound, biblical thinking. Evaluating my subconscious myths, I continued to discover huge "cracks" in my belief system that enabled me to change my ruling passion and direct my actions in an honorable fashion. My values were changed to reflect biblical truths.

- *I cannot always be in control of every situation in my life.* Because I still live in this imperfect world, my security will continue to be rocked by changes involving possessions, circumstances, and people.
- *Just because God does not alleviate my current pain does not mean He does not love me.* The apostle Paul's pain definitely was not alleviated, and yet he wrote,

We've been surrounded and battered by troubles, but we're not demoralized; we're not sure what to do, but we know that God knows what to do. . . . So we're not giving up. . . . Even though on the outside it often looks like things are falling apart on us, on the inside, where God is making new life, not a day goes by without his unfolding grace. These hard times are small potatoes compared to the coming good times, the lavish celebration prepared for us. There's far more than meets the eye. The things we see now are here today, gone tomorrow. But the things we can't see now will last forever. (2 Corinthians 4: 8-9,16-18, MSG)

- *Admitting my doubts about God to someone else is not a sin.*
  Jackie Hudson writes,

Christians who are struggling with doubt don't talk about it. They are ashamed of it. Or they have resigned themselves to living with it like they would an annoying headache. Tragically, many Christians today quickly label doubt as "sin" or "unbelief." This adds guilt to the believer's already painful battle, and the condition worsens. For a sensitive "doubter" the struggle can be nearly intolerable.[1]

Changes we view as negative often affect our relationship with God and our feelings toward Him. We are not heretics if we have doubts about Him, but *we do need to be able to talk to someone about those doubts.*

THE FIRM BASE FOR SECURITY AND JOY

We can count on three things that will last forever: God, His Word, and His people. Our financial security, job situation, marital status, or health could change tomorrow—but some things *are* eternal. Malachi 3:6 says, "I the LORD do not change." Wow! That gives all of us a sense of security. Everything around us may change, but *our God is changeless!*

Besides God Himself, we have access to the emotional and spiritual support of Christian people around us. For those of us from the "I'll do it myself" mentality, it's a big step of growth to allow someone to help us—through physically assisting us or by giving us wise counsel.

In Exodus there's a story about a battle between the Israelites and the

Amalekites. When Moses held up his hands, the Israelites were winning, but whenever he lowered his hands, the other side started winning. We read in the Old Testament account: "When Moses' hands grew tired, they took a stone and put it under him and he sat on it. Aaron and Hur held his hands up—one on one side, one on the other—so that his hands remained steady till sunset" (Exodus 17:12). Aaron and Hur were support people who gave physical, emotional, and spiritual help to Moses in his hour of need. Who won the battle? The Israelites—it was a winning team!

When we face major changes as Christian women, there *are* people who can "come alongside."

THE DOOR TO OPPORTUNITY

When our actions reflect ruling passions that are based on biblical convictions rather than on distortions of the truth, our change points become opportunities for showcasing the power of God.

Is it possible to adapt to change joyfully? Tim Hansel thinks so. He says,

Joy is a process, a journey—often muffled, sometimes detoured;
a mystery in which we participate, not a product we can grasp.
It grows and regenerates as we have the courage to let go and
trust the process. Growth and joy are inhibited when we say "if
only," enhanced when we realize that failures and difficulties are
not only a critical part of the process, but are our very opportunities to grow.[2]

Thanks, Tim! I need to remember that! Our lives are constantly changing, and with those changes many new opportunities and problems are emerging. Whether the change is one we have chosen or is one that we have no control over, it can be the door to an exciting adventure through which God can reshape the course of our lives.

PART FOUR:

The Passion for Intimacy

CHAPTER 7

Please Hear Me!:
To Experience Human Connection

*We are born helpless. As soon as we are fully
conscious we discover loneliness. We need
others physically, emotionally, intellectually;
we need them if we are to know
anything, even ourselves.*

C. S. LEWIS

KATE HESITATED at the door of a local restaurant and then went in.
The hostess led her to a window booth and placed a large menu
in her hands. Sunbeams danced on the tabletop, begging to be recognized
with a cheery response, but she wasn't in the mood.

Glancing around, she saw two women at the next table engrossed in
a captivating discussion. Kate couldn't hear the actual conversation, but
the body language said it all. The women were leaning toward each other,
as if they were sharing important news. Their eye contact spoke of trust,
interest, concern, love, and deep care. While one woman spoke, the other
nodded, indicating intense listening. Occasional outbursts of laughter
were a reminder that the lunch these women enjoyed was more than a
serious meeting—it was a celebration of friendship! As they left the

restaurant, they hugged briefly, and Kate overheard one say to the other, "I'll call you tomorrow!"

As Kate sat there, the loneliness she'd been experiencing too often swept over her like a rushing tide. These women had the kind of friendship Kate longed for but didn't have. Her sense of emptiness and isolation was like a gnawing ache that wouldn't leave. Bit by bit it was wearing away Kate's sense of connectedness and eroding her ability to think rationally. She felt tormented with the repeated internal message: *I'm alone. Other people can develop and maintain friendships, but I can't. The woman I most desire to have as my friend doesn't reciprocate. There must be a flaw in my personality that alienates me from people I want to be close to. There is no one I can call right now who cares about communicating with me at an intimate level.*

I had met Kate at a Christian leadership conference. Her list of credentials was enviable; at the time of our meeting she was traveling internationally for her church denomination.

She had classic good looks—from her perfectly styled haircut to her professionally manicured fingernails to her polished pumps. Her quick wit was balanced nicely with enough intelligence to give her "unstuffy" credibility. She deeply loved the Lord and had committed her life to Christian work. We "clicked" well during the conference and began writing to each other shortly thereafter. Occasionally she visited in my home, and during one of those visits she shared her intense struggle.

Kate's Expectation: She expected to share in a mutually satisfying "kindred-spirit" friendship with Anne, a woman she selected as the person she would most like to be close to. They lived in the same city and Kate felt the physical closeness was an added benefit for phoning each other frequently and spending time together.

Kate's Disappointment: After choosing Anne to be her special friend, she spent months investing her time and resources into developing the relationship. She invited her to lunch, sent her "no-special-occasion" greeting cards with warm sentiments, attended the piano recital of Anne's daughter, called her several times a week, and remembered important days with flowers and gifts. Later, when Anne was asked to direct the church Christmas program, Kate volunteered her time to put the program on her computer for easy corrections and access; then she assisted by caring for Anne's children during the program rehearsals.

As time went on, Kate realized that Anne was always grateful for her thoughtful gestures and was always warm and caring in her responses, but the relationship was one-sided. Kate shared her problems, challenges, and dreams, and Anne listened and seemed to care, but she never related any of her own innermost heartaches and longings. Kate sent cards and notes, but Anne didn't. Kate phoned and Anne was gracious, but usually Anne was not the initiator of the call. Anne made time for Kate when she "showed up," but Anne never pursued spending time with Kate. As one incident was stacked on another, Kate grew deeply disappointed.

Kate's Longing: Kate's heartfelt longing was for *human connection,* for the intimacy of a friendship that would be mutually satisfying. Her heart sought a friend who would genuinely like her, find her intelligent, and desire sharing at a deep level. Kate's longing for the "togetherness" of a caring companion began consuming her thoughts.

Kate's Emotions: Her initial emotion was anger. After pouring so much time and effort into a relationship, she felt she deserved more. The anger quickly swung to fear—fear that if Anne cut her off completely, she would have no one. Then Kate's emotions would bounce back to anger at this woman who was not opening up to her.

Kate's Belief System: Kate should have realized that as a Christian woman, her deepest longing for intimacy would never totally be met by another person, but her convictions and values had become warped over the years. She truly believed she was one of only a few people who longed for a close friendship and didn't have one. Her highest priority became easing her pain of rejection, and the actions that followed were a testimony to her faulty thinking.

Kate's Ruling Passion: If Kate's convictions had been rooted in her deep personal knowledge of the Bible, she would have chosen a ruling passion that would have allowed God Himself to fill the vacancy—perhaps through a different friend, or by a surprising change in Anne, or by a new intimacy with Him. She could have chosen to experience a greater fulfillment by offering her loneliness to Him instead of trying to take care of her own deep longing. But her instinctive drive was to lessen her own distress.

Kate's Action: Initially, Kate's choice was reflected by an action of total withdrawal from Anne, without an explanation. When Anne contacted her by phone to ask if she was all right, Kate's pent-up emotions exploded in a torrential outpouring of anger toward Anne. She pushed Anne further away than she'd ever been before.

If Kate's actions had ended there it would have been bad enough, but she immediately focused on another person to befriend in her desperate attempt to satisfy her need for intimacy. This time she was less patient and became demanding in the relationship. By the time Kate talked to me, she had already destroyed four different relationships with women she had at one time wanted as her close friends.

INTIMACY DEFINED

Intimacy is a close relationship that results from careful study of the other person.

To be close to another person in a friendship or marital relationship, we need to know him/her personally and experience "connectedness" with that individual in several areas.

- *Intellectual intimacy* makes us feel understood. Someone has the ability to reason with us on our intellectual level and there are "sparks" of enlightenment and stimulation during our conversations.
- *Emotional intimacy* is the strong *feeling* we have for someone else.

Usually the emotion is love and it gives us the connectedness of being tenderly cared for and totally accepted. Emotional intimacy doesn't always need words to be expressed. A hug, a squeeze of the arm, a touch of the hand, or a look can deeply express this type of intimacy. When we experience it, we feel cherished.

- *Social intimacy* allows us to feel like "part of the group." We join church groups, sports clubs, neighborhood gatherings, Bible study organizations, civic clubs, worthy causes, and business associations. Our mutual interest, work, or involvement brings us together with people of like passions, persuasions, and interests.

- *Cultural intimacy* makes us feel joined to people who share our roots, nationality, traditions, or values. Sometimes we meet people for the first time and sense peak-level communication because of our similar backgrounds.

- *Spiritual intimacy* can be ours on two levels: first, a personal relationship with the God who created us, loves us, and cares for us; and second, a spiritual bonding with individuals who share a similar passion for God, His Word, and accomplishing His work on the earth. There is an initial connectedness that stems from like faith in God, but true spiritual bonding evolves as a result of tracking each other's spiritual journeys, holding each other accountable for growth, and joining together to reach our world for Christ and lead people to spiritual maturity.

For me, an intimate friendship is a relationship with another person that involves many of the following elements:

1. A deep care and concern for me personally
2. A personality I enjoy (intelligence, spiritual depth, and a great sense of humor are a few traits I'd be seeking)
3. An active interest in and support of my projects and dreams

4. An instinct to automatically come alongside and help when I am in need

5. A spiritual bonding as friends (hard to define, but your heart tells you when you have it)

6. An "instant availability" when true emergencies demand momentary inconvenience

7. A commitment to each other, while allowing the other person to enjoy the freedom of time alone, other friendships, and individual personhood

Here's where Kate had a problem. She admitted it was very difficult for her to accept the fact that Anne had a deeper need for time alone than she did. Anne had difficulty functioning in her many busy activities without a daily block of time for solitude. Anne also had a personality that drew many close friends, and Kate was easily threatened when she overheard Anne speak with deep warmth and concern to someone else.

8. A compassionate heart that cheers when I succeed and feels my pain when I fail

9. A tangible support through communication (often enough so I feel valued, but infrequently enough so I don't feel strangled)

This is an area where Kate failed repeatedly in her pursuit of an intimate friendship. She called too often, sent gifts that were too large, and showed up on the doorstep so often that Anne began feeling pushed into the "friendship." Kate's lavish outpouring of time and attention was always a mixed blessing. She helped in many meaningful areas, but always left Anne feeling a little guilty for not bonding with her as an "only" best friend. There was something about Kate's desperate need for her that made Anne back off instead of come closer. True "kindred-spirit" friendship cannot exist when two people do not approach each other as people of equal worth and value.

10. An ability to lovingly confront me with hard questions that hold me accountable for spiritual growth and personal integrity

Kate shared her failings and spiritual frustrations with Anne, hoping that Anne would do the same and that their mutual sharing of secrets would bond them. In her desire for a close "accountability" relationship with Anne, she had difficulty waiting for the right timing. She found herself spilling out her heart in an emotional "child/parent" fashion, rather than allowing herself and Anne to grow closer as adults who had similar struggles and temptations.

11. A listening ear—someone *attentive* who will really *hear* me
12. A heart for God's Word and an eager interest in ministry-related activities
13. A powerful prayer partner ———
14. An affirming encourager
15. An individual who can expect all of the above from me without making me feel the "weight" of obligation if I don't measure up

Although both Kate and Anne were single, there was a difference. Anne was a widow with two children, and Kate had never been married. Kate's traveling ministry with her church denomination was very demanding when she was out of town, but her days were quite free when she got back from a trip. She felt a need for sharing with a close friend and for relaxation with someone else during those breaks. On the other hand, Anne's busy life of part-time work, carpooling for her children's activities, responsibilities with a neighborhood Bible study, and being chairwoman of a Christian Women's Club were time-consuming on a daily basis. When Anne was simply too busy with other commitments to be in touch, Kate misinterpreted Anne's lack of communication as lack of interest.

WE NEED EACH OTHER

Do *you* have someone in your life that meets the qualifications of a friend I listed in the previous section? My list may be somewhat unrealistic if used as a checklist for potential friends, but it's good for me to mentally review these characteristics. It helps me to evaluate if I've been taking more from others than I've been giving back.

All human beings have a different "comfort zone" when it comes to being close to other people. Some, like Kate, enjoy being surrounded with people most of the time; others, like Anne, feel suffocated if they don't have their own space at regular intervals.

Many experts in communication are now saying that the average person needs at least twelve touches a day to feel loved, cared for, and significant. Regardless of our "comfort zone" differences, the fact remains—we really do *need* each other desperately! Even those who don't seem to have a big desire for *physical touch* need to be held with an *emotional touch*. The human race cries out—sometimes nonverbally, but still with poignant urgency— *"Please hold me!"* and *"Please hear me."*

UNDERSTANDING LONELINESS

The need people have for human connection has been screaming at us in recent years with the rise in suicides. Jan Fawcett, in a publication titled *Before It's Too Late*, says,

> In studies of human traits that often lead to suicide, three words
> crop up again and again: loss, loneliness and hopelessness. In
> many cases, an actual loss is involved—the loss of a parent
> through death, the breakup of a marriage, the loss of a job, the
> loss of health. . . . Hopelessness . . . is perhaps the deepest reflec-
> tion of despair. When things are bad, people are encouraged by

the belief that they will get better. . . . Loneliness and despair are frequently the result of loss and depression.[1]

Being lonely is the empty, aching experience of being alone and isolated. When we're lonesome, we have a desolate, unhappy feeling when no one else is with us. Sometimes we're just as lonely when someone else is around if there is no emotional, intellectual, or spiritual intimacy in the relationship. Proverbs 13:12 (MSG) says, "Unrelenting disappointment leaves you heartsick, but a sudden good break can turn life around." When we hope for the intimacy of friendship and the longing is not met, we can actually feel ill.

Solitude is aloneness that we *choose.* It's pre-selected time set apart for thinking, reading, spiritual renewal, or "regrouping." It can be the wonderful experience of "getting the wind back in our sails." Loneliness, on the other hand, is a type of suffering that comes from a lack of intimacy. Loneliness cuts like a sharp knife; when we see happy people interact with each other in intimate ways, the knife is twisted and the pain becomes deeper.

Someone placed this ad in a Kansas newspaper: "I will listen to you talk for thirty minutes without comment for five dollars." Did anybody call? You bet! Soon the individual was receiving ten to twenty calls a day. The pang of loneliness was so sharp that many people were willing to pay to talk to another human being for half an hour.

INTIMATE FRIENDSHIP—THE WAY IT USED TO BE!

Perhaps the most extraordinary example of human friendship in Scripture is the intimate relationship between David and Jonathan. At the beginning of 1 Samuel 18, Saul was king of Israel. David had recently killed Goliath, and he and Saul's son Jonathan had become friends. The prophet Samuel had anointed David, not Jonathan, to succeed Saul as king when Saul died.

Jonathan and David entered a covenant relationship as friends. A covenant was the most solemn, binding agreement that could be made between two people—covenants dated back to the days of Abraham. The description of what took place and the language used in this passage make the close relationship between these two men very clear to us:

> Jonathan became one in spirit with David, and he loved him as himself. And Jonathan made a covenant with David because he loved him as himself. Jonathan took off the robe he was wearing and gave it to David, along with his tunic, and even his sword, his bow and his belt. (1 Samuel 18:1,3-4)

In Old Testament times there were no legal documents as we know them today, and there was an unusual custom of "cutting" a covenant that made an agreement binding. Individuals entering into a covenant relationship with each other would exchange their coats or robes as well as their girdles (belts). For most of us, a girdle is a device used to keep an unfortunate situation from spreading, but in the days of David and Jonathan, it was something worn around the hips as a symbol of security. Then they would exchange swords. It was like saying, "Everything I am and have I am giving to you because I love you. You take my enemies and I'll take yours. If anyone comes after you, they'll have to take me on, too. You are my friend."

After this they took an animal and literally hacked it down the middle. Half of the animal was placed on one side of the men with the other half on the other side. After walking in a figure eight around the animal, they stood in the middle, pointed to heaven and then to the animal, and said, "God do so to me if I break this covenant."

This sounds gruesome to me as I read about it in twenty-first century America, but David and Jonathan were making an important point. It was like they were saying, "The intimate friendship relationship we have is more than a passing emotional commitment. It's binding, permanent, and absolutely undissolvable; I am committed to you."

The next step was to make a small cut in their wrists and mingle their blood. Then powder or dirt was placed on the wound to make sure a scar would develop. From that point on, every time they raised their hands to greet someone or to give a blessing, people would view the scar and know they had a covenant partner. The scar was also a reminder to love, defend, and protect their dearest friend.

The covenant partners then exchanged names and gave a statement of the covenant terms. They said, "All my assets are yours . . . and my debts are yours, too." They ate a memorial meal together and then planted a memorial to the covenant. Usually this was a tree that would stand as a constant reminder of the seriousness of their commitment to each other.

WHAT DOES THIS MEAN TO ME?

This old custom of "covenant" is a picture of the intimate friendship relationship that's ours because of Jesus Christ. One day I went through every step in the whole process of the covenant agreement and pictured the personalization of God's love for me . . . and I wept.

When Jesus came to earth, He exchanged His heavenly garment for human flesh. Jesus has become my Defender—if the Enemy attacks me, it's as if he's attacking my God: "The one who is in you is greater than the one who is in the world" (1 John 4:4). Jesus "cut" the covenant by giving His life on the cross of Calvary, and the scars in His hands are a permanent reminder of His sacrifice. In Isaiah 49:16 we read, "I have engraved you on the palms of my hands."

He's given me a new name—Christian—and then He says, "All my assets are yours." They are listed in Galatians 5:22: "But the fruit of the Spirit is love, joy, peace, patience, kindness, goodness, faithfulness, gentleness and self-control."

Today, every time I take communion, it's a reminder of my intimate relationship with Christ. Communion is a memorial of His sacrifice on the cross for me. When I am alone—not in solitude of my own choosing, but in times of loneliness—I try to remember that I am in an intimate, everlasting, tenacious relationship with Him!

There are moments in our lives when loneliness knocks at our door and walks in—the uninvited guest who will not leave on demand. Then unexpected emotions come as our disappointments create longings for what we see in the lives of others. For Kate, loneliness came when she saw two friends in a restaurant enjoying the type of relationship she wanted. Sometimes loneliness comes when we hear a testimony of someone who is close to God, and we don't know Him or we feel far from Him.

Elisabeth Elliot has known widowhood twice. Her first husband, Jim, was killed by the Auca Indians on the mission field in Ecuador. Addison Leitch, Presbyterian professor at Gordon-Conwell Seminary, was her second husband. He died a slow, painful death by cancer and Elisabeth was alone—again! In her book titled *Loneliness,* she says,

> Loneliness comes over us sometimes as a sudden tide. It is one
> of the terms of our humanness, and, in a sense, therefore, incurable. Yet I have found peace in my loneliest times not only
> through acceptance of the situation, but through making it an
> offering to God, who can transfigure it into something for the
> good of others.[2]

Our basic need for intimacy first must be met in experiencing a personal relationship with God Himself by accepting Jesus Christ as our personal Savior. From that point on, additional needs for "human connection" may come from friends, family, or a spouse. But in many moments when people disappoint us—and they will—we still have a Covenant Partner who says, "I will never leave you nor forsake you."

INTIMACY — THE STEALERS

In most cases we are the roadblock to our own connection with other people. Psychologists say there are several factors that keep us from being close to people.

VIEWING OURSELVES AS UNLOVABLE

When we feel unattractive or "dumb" compared to others, we have trouble believing that anyone would want to be close to us. When we don't feel like a person of equal worth in a relationship, there is no possibility for true friendship.

HAVING UNREALISTIC EXPECTATIONS OF SOMEONE ELSE

Our personal dream of a close relationship may cause us to demand much more of another person than he or she might be able to give. It causes us deep disappointment and is a constant frustration to the other person.

BEING TOO BUSY

Our days are much busier than they've ever been before. Intimate relationships take time. Most of us want closeness without the investment of attention to the other person and the "togetherness" necessary for intimacy.

STRUGGLING WITH POOR COMMUNICATION SKILLS

Some of us *feel* deeply, but we have great difficulty *telling* someone else our heartfelt emotions. If we don't ever voice our needs, hurts, joys, and dreams to others, we limit the potential closeness. Family background has a lot to do with this. People who grew up in a family that talked, touched, and laughed together find communicating at an intimate level much easier than people who were raised by "non-touchers" who didn't voice their affection and opinions.

COMPARING OUR SITUATION WITH "THE IDEAL"

Women who do not have a strong family support system sometimes admit that it's easy to look with envy at families that *seem* to have so much going for them. On the surface it may *look* like someone we know has the ideal husband, the perfect children, supportive siblings, or committed friends, but that's not always true. In a roundabout way our disappointment leads to a longing for what we *think* others have, and it often leads to envy and depression.

THE COST AND THE RESPONSIBILITY OF INTIMACY

No Happy without pain

The intimacy I enjoy with my extended family and friends is sometimes deep, intense, passionate, and painful. At times the closeness opens me to hurt that I could have avoided if I hadn't opened my heart to those I love.

Intimacy in relationships opens me to emotional pain and fills me with joy beyond description. It's a paradox that defies explanation. My big responsibility is to quit trying to change other people to fit my definition of "friend." As I accept their differences, my life is more complete.

As I commit myself to the person and to the relationship, the fear of being rejected is reduced and eventually disappears. In conflicts I'm able to accept that we will never think exactly alike—and that's all right. I let go of my demands for the "perfect friend of my imagined dreams." I learn to celebrate our differences while giving my friend "breathing room." Intimacy blossoms best when it isn't smothered.

A PERSONAL CHALLENGE

We need to realize that although we have deep needs for intimacy, we can also become "emotional filling stations" for other people. Taking the time to listen to people while giving them sincere, caring eye contact is a beginning. There should be a desire within us to provide personal concern and helpful resources to others, and even more important, lead them to the source of completeness—a covenant relationship with God Himself!

When we struggle with loneliness, we shouldn't be surprised. Life is filled with "alone" times. Through prayer, we can make our loneliness an offering to God. Instead of hibernating in our grief, we can get involved in the lives of other people. In the middle of our disappointments, we can choose a ruling passion that is honorable and holy.

Intimacy costs top dollar and is never available in the bargain basement. It means time—to listen, to talk, to play, to pray, to ponder.

Reread the fifteen characteristics of a friend that were listed on pages 101-103. Prayerfully consider the people in your life now. Who is it God wants you to reach out to at this time? It will take personal sacrifice, time, and energy, but the rewards are great. Remember the truth of Proverbs 27:17: "As iron sharpens iron, so one man sharpens another." Are you actively involved in someone else's life, stimulating him or her to excellence?

C. S. Lewis described intimacy with others this way:

To love at all is to be vulnerable. Love anything, and your heart will certainly be wrung and possibly be broken. If you want to make sure of keeping it intact, you must give your heart to no one. . . . Wrap it carefully with hobbies and little luxuries; avoid all entanglements; lock it up safe in a casket . . . of your own selfishness. . . . (There) it will not be broken: it will become unbreakable, impenetrable, irredeemable.[3]

My challenge to you is this: Take the time to develop intimacy with other people. The risk is well worth the pain! You can count on it.

CHAPTER 8

Please Hold Me!:
To Be Sexually Fulfilled

*It is difficult to define love. But we may say
that in the soul, it is a ruling passion; in
the mind, it is a close sympathy and affinity;
in the body, a wholly secret and delicate
longing to possess what we love.*
DUC DE LA ROCHEFOUCAULD

THE WOMAN stood, moved to the center aisle, and walked to the front of the auditorium where I was standing. Bursting into tears, she fell into my arms and blurted out, "I'm an adulteress!"

I had just finished presenting the last message at a women's retreat and had indicated that if any women in the audience wanted to stay for a time of prayer, I would be happy to remain and meet them in the front of the room. The biblical challenge I chose to focus on had come from Genesis 39. I shared the account of Joseph resisting the heavy, repeated sexual temptation of Potiphar's wife in Egypt.

Through the woman's sobs, she shared her story: "I'm having an affair with the husband of my best friend. We go to the same church, and I'm her roommate at this retreat. I can't go on living like this!"

AN ISOLATED CASE?

Two weeks later I was sitting at my kitchen table finishing breakfast when the phone rang. I picked up the receiver, greeted the caller, and soon recognized a desperate tone in the woman's voice. "Carol, I don't know if you remember meeting me, but I need help. I thought you might be willing to talk to me. It's something very personal. Could I come to your home?"

The woman had come a long distance, but she arrived on my doorstep at the appointed hour. I liked her immediately. Her appearance and demeanor made a positive statement of intelligence, warmth, and spiritual sensitivity. We shared a bit of small talk. Nancy was married, the mother of three lovely children, and a very active church worker. I wondered what possible major problem a woman like this could have.

I paused momentarily, made lingering eye contact, and said, "Nancy, tell me, why are you here?" Her eyes brimmed with tears and soon her story came rushing out with the force and speed of a breaking dam.

Nancy married young and had children right away. She loved her husband and her life, but as the children grew, her husband became more and more involved with his work. She immersed herself in church activities and soon joined the choir. Dave, the choir director, was the husband of one of Nancy's good friends. Their children got along well together and the families often paired up at church activities.

Her emotions erupted like a volcano as she blurted out, "I honestly don't know how it happened. Maybe I was flirting a bit during choir rehearsals. Maybe I was lonely because my husband spends so much time at work. I've even wondered if I just wanted a little variety in my life . . . but it happened. Dave and I began meeting for a quick cup of coffee, as friends, following the rehearsals. It all seemed so innocent. Our families were best friends. . . ."

By the time Nancy got into her story, I realized this woman was on the verge of losing her husband—after eighteen years of marriage! Dave and Nancy's relationship began innocently enough, but soon their post-rehearsal choir dates turned into conversations in which they were verbally pointing out the flaws in their spouses.

For a while they only mentally reviewed the positive qualities in each other. But soon they began complimenting each other on personal character traits and attractiveness. On the days of choir rehearsals, Nancy found herself thinking about what she would wear that Dave would find attractive. She looked forward to his approving glance as she took her place among the sopranos.

Later when they had dessert and coffee, he bowed for a quick prayer of thanks for the food. He lightly touched her hand during the prayer and she flushed a bit, finally admitting to herself how much she enjoyed being physically close to him. It didn't take long for the "lingering coffee shop dates" to turn into a full-blown affair. I listened and then asked, "Nancy, how long has this been going on?"

Choking back the sobs, she muttered, "Off and on for *five years*." I tried not to look startled. She continued, "Many times in the last few years Dave and I have both confessed our sin to God, and we have stayed away from each other for months at a time. We've gone forward in church. Several times we thought our problem was behind us. Now we've been caught. My husband found out; he told Dave's wife, and now two marriages are about to be destroyed. Both Dave and I love our spouses, and we are sick about the pain we've inflicted on our families. Do you think there is any hope for us?"

Nancy suddenly looked up. With urgency in her voice she stated, "I still can't understand *how* this could have happened. I'm a Christian. What I've been doing is against everything I've ever been taught. I've been somewhat disappointed in my marriage—not *cherished* the way I'd like—but I've been *reasonably* happy."

I listened as Nancy described the progressive breakdown in her intimate communication with her husband, her growing attraction to someone else, and its ultimate progression into a physical relationship. Over the next couple of hours, I intermittently asked more questions: "What led up to this immoral relationship? What were the danger signs? Why do you think it happened? Why did it continue after repeated confessions to God and numerous decisions to quit?"

She honestly didn't know. "Nancy," I said, "tell me about your thought life. What do you think about when your mind is not occupied with the urgencies of life? Have you ever had a problem with fantasizing about other men? What's the last thing on your mind when you go to bed at night and the first thing you think about when you wake up in the morning?"

With ease she responded. "Just normal fantasies. . . . I like to imagine what it's like to be in the arms of a gentle, tender, compassionate, intelligent, and attractive Christian man. Through my early married years I often thought about what it would be like to be physically close to my pastor or other Christian men I respected. I knew my thoughts couldn't hurt anyone else, and my dream world helped me to survive some of the more boring aspects of housekeeping duties."

Nancy soon admitted that the choir director she had become involved with had been the main object of her "imaginings" for many months before she stepped over the line into a physical relationship. The problem was not the product of one weak moment of temptation. It was the result of years of practicing an immoral thought life. And she had never considered that it was sin.

As she sat in my home, safely removed from familiar faces, her "walls" came down and she openly revealed the disappointment in her own marriage and her longing for meaningful intellectual, emotional, spiritual, and physical intimacy from a caring spouse. It soon became obvious that Nancy's fantasies were not simply the result of being attracted to someone else, but of a severe lack of intimacy in her own marriage.

Nancy's Expectation: She believed that marriage to a Christian man would mean living in a happy and fulfilling emotional, sexual, spiritual, and intellectual relationship with her best friend. Nancy expected the intellectual intimacy of her courtship to continue after the wedding. She realized her husband did not grow up in a family that expressed physical affection very often, but in her optimism she was sure that would change after the wedding. She expected to marry a tender lover who would combine a caring touch, affirming words, a clean body, and a deep physical desire for her alone!

Nancy's Disappointment: Bill was an excellent breadwinner and always took care of the financial needs of the family, but early in the marriage there was a breakdown in the physical intimacy in their relationship. Every night after dinner they watched television, and Bill, exhausted from a demanding job, fell asleep on the couch soon after the news. Nancy felt rejected on many levels. Caring for small children all day left her starved for intellectual, emotional, and spiritual communication with her husband. When he hurriedly approached her for physical intimacy without first meeting her emotional needs, she was more than disappointed.

Nancy's Longing: Nancy's deep disappointment led to a longing for a close, loving relationship that would make her feel understood, emotionally needed, important, secure, physically attractive, and singly cherished. She longed for the sexual act of marriage to be the culmination of an intimate relationship on many other levels. Nancy believed that what she wanted was God's ideal for marriage.

Nancy's Emotions: When months passed and Bill's behavior didn't change, she felt "used" when he made love to her without first meeting her need for positive communication. His sexual advances stirred a progression of emotions: first, fear that her life would be miserable in many ways; second, anger that her husband seemed oblivious to her real needs. Finally, she was churning with desire for emotional, spiritual, and physical closeness with someone who would *hear* and *hold* her.

Nancy's Belief System: She knew the Bible taught that marriage was a sacred trust between two people, and she knew she *did* love Bill. However, her convictions were clouded with distorted values as her thoughts lingered on her unhappiness, loneliness, and isolation. The damage to her spiritual judgment made her own fulfillment her highest priority—and she made choices that reflected her flawed thinking.

Nancy's *Ruling Passion:* Fueled by her daily habit of immoral thinking, which she considered "harmless fantasizing," her belief system had become warped. If her values had been firmly based on God's Word, she would have been able to channel her need for romance and meaningful physical intimacy into a love willing to live with pain while she worked on a godly solution. Instead, she most valued being free of the anguish of not being cherished and decided on a negative ruling passion.

Nancy's *Action:* Her resulting behavior was the outcome of her ruling passion. She began mentally listing the negative characteristics of her husband while focusing on the opposite positive characteristics of Dave. Anticipating the choir rehearsals and the coffee shop chats afterward, Nancy began dressing to please Dave. She verbally complimented him on his clothing and accomplishments with the music program in the church. Reading "sexual innuendos" into friendly hugs and casual touches, Nancy spent her time fantasizing about romantic encounters with Dave. When they were alone, she told him of her intense loneliness at home and her deep attraction for him. A comforting hug led to a caress, which led to an embrace, which soon led to his bed.

"MOI? I'M A CHRISTIAN—IT COULDN'T HAPPEN TO ME!"

The highly publicized romance of Kermit the Frog and Miss Piggy brings to mind the visual image of the gorgeous, voluptuous Miss Piggy batting her eyelashes at the camera in complete surprise while she purses her curvaceous lips and asks her most famous question, using her *only* French vocabulary word: "Moi?"

Sadly, I could fill this entire book with more true accounts of similar situations. In the last several years I have found myself counseling more and more Christian women in immoral, adulterous relationships with Christian men. Almost all of them thought it could never happen to them. Most of these women knew the spouses of the married men they slept with. Many of them love their own husbands.

The reaction of surprise that most women express when they experience adultery is much like the three-year-old's explanation for being in the kitchen, standing on a chair, eating cookies when his mother walks in: "I just climbed up to smell them and my tooth got caught."

By denying our deepest longings and pushing back our intense, passionate desire for intimacy, we wind up with actions that surprise us. Our emotions course through us, demanding romance, adventure, and "love"—and in our "innocence" (which is really denial), we're often surprised that we're capable of a negative ruling passion that results in the sinful act of adultery.

I have a little of "Miss Piggy" in me. Sometimes I'm all dressed up and I've curled my eyelashes and put on my high heels. I then flash my smile around to mask my deep insecurities and longing for intimacy, and I forget who I really am. In spite of all the Hollywood makeup, Miss Piggy still has a snout and she's still a pig! And no matter how much I'd like to believe that I'm a Christian woman of such maturity that I'd never stoop to immoral fantasies or to a sexual experience outside of my marriage, I need to remember—I still have a depraved, sinful nature at war with my new nature. When wrong thoughts linger, I so quickly gesture with a hand to my chest as I innocently query: "Moi?"

A BIBLICAL PERSPECTIVE

A few years ago I had the privilege of working as director of women's ministries at a church in Fort Wayne, Indiana. In any large church there are numerous couples with marriage problems, and it was a help to have Dr. Ken Nichols on our staff as the church psychologist. Ken often led marriage enrichment seminars, and his basic statement on physical intimacy was this: "Properly experienced within marriage and its commitment to fidelity, the sexual union brings a sense of well-being, complete identity, joy unbounded, perfect mutuality, freedom in responsibility, fulfillment of purpose, and an indescribable unity of being."

Most of us heartily agree with that statement. But even as I read it and do a mental checklist of my own physical experience of married love, I realize it's an *ideal* picture of sexual intimacy as God intended it to be—not the reality of my life! Often God's pattern is forgotten as we juggle home pressures, hormones, unexpected company, church responsibilities, and job stresses. But in spite of my imperfections and interruptions, *God does have an ideal.*

GOD IS THE AUTHOR OF SEX.

In Genesis 2:24-25 we read, "For this reason a man will leave his father and mother and be united to his wife, and they will become one flesh. The man and his wife were both naked, and they felt no shame." The primary meaning of "one flesh" refers to the sexual act.

God is the manufacturer of sex. It was created by God, sanctioned in the Garden of Eden, and meant to provide unity, intimacy, and pleasure. But because of the world's perversion of something so beautiful, many Christians have almost become embarrassed to discuss the subject of sexual intimacy.

GOD CREATED SEX TO BE PLEASURABLE.

There are many subjects where the Bible speaks for itself very clearly, and physical intimacy is one of those subjects.

Old Jewish law stated, "If a man has recently married, he must not be sent to war or have any other duty laid on him. For one year he is to be free to stay at home and bring happiness to the wife he has married" (Deuteronomy 24:5). The inference in that verse does not indicate that he should be sitting around telling jokes for a year, but that he should be learning the intricacies of bringing physical pleasure to his wife.

The entire book of Song of Songs reveals the joy that should be experienced in the physical relationship of marriage. "His left arm is under my head, and his right arm embraces me" (Song of Songs 2:6). Solomon's description of his "beautiful darling" in chapter 4:1-7 is enough to make me blush. This man is in love! He continues in verses 9-11: "You have stolen my heart, my sister, my bride; you have stolen my heart with one glance of your eyes. . . . How much more pleasing is your love than wine, and the fragrance of your perfume than any spice! Your lips drop sweetness as the honeycomb."

There's no doubt about it. God intended the act of physical, sexual love in marriage to be pleasurable.

GOD EXPECTS US TO MEET OUR MATE'S NEEDS.

Another major biblical teaching involves the responsibility of meeting each other's sexual needs:

> It's good for a man to have a wife, and for a woman to have a husband. Sexual drives are strong, but marriage is strong enough to contain them and provide for a balanced and fulfilling sexual life in a world of sexual disorder. The marriage bed must be a place of mutuality—the husband seeking to satisfy his wife, the wife seeking to satisfy her husband. . . . Marriage is a decision to serve the other, whether in bed or out. Abstaining from sex is permissible for a period of time if you both agree to it, and if it's for the purposes of prayer and fasting—but only for such times. Then come back together again. Satan has an ingenious way of tempting us when we least expect it. (1 Corinthians 7:2-5, MSG)

Occasionally I meet a Christian woman who is devout in her practice of church attendance and Bible reading, but her husband isn't. Her way of responding to him is to read her Bible and pray ostentatiously in front of him and then deprive him of physical intimacy with her. She is using his desire for sex to manipulate him. Sometimes she does this with a series of excuses or even by the use of blatant rudeness. At other times she physically allows him to "use" her body, while acting totally uninterested and unfulfilled herself. It's as if she's saying, "God says I have to comply, so let's get it over with!" When we respond in this way, we defeat our own desire to reach our spouse for Christ. We also rob ourselves of the very intimacy our heart strongly desires.

GOD CREATED SEX TO BE EXPERIENCED WITHIN MARRIAGE, NOT APART FROM IT.

In the opening story, Nancy's decision to seek relief from her loneliness by having an affair with Dave brought intense grief to her life and threatened the stability of her family. The Bible gives clear guidelines and warnings regarding the physical expression of love with someone other than our own spouse. Hebrews 13:4 (MSG) says, "Honor marriage, and guard the sacredness of sexual intimacy between wife and husband. God draws a firm line against casual and illicit sex."

In all my years of working with women, I have never heard anyone say, "The best thing that ever happened to me was the day I gave in to temptation and had an affair with a man I cared deeply about!" Even when a woman verbally expresses feelings of love toward the object of her physical passion, she usually admits that her immoral relationship has brought pain, confusion, guilt, spiritual failure, inner agony, and suffering to other people she loves.

UNFULFILLED EXPECTATIONS

All of us who choose to marry come to the altar with a hope chest full of expectations. We see our bridegroom at the end of the aisle in his perfectly pressed tuxedo, and our dreams are full of romance and passion. We anticipate excitement, unrestrained sensuousness, and chivalric deeds. But disappointments mount quickly when we realize that marriage to Prince Charming means cleaning up after his horse!

If we don't marry, we sometimes wonder if sexual intimacy is the epitome of all happiness and fulfillment on earth. If we do marry, we often wonder if this "intimacy in marriage" would be what it's supposed to be if we'd married somebody else. It doesn't take long for the Miss Piggy in all of us to see that Kermit is not a frog prince—he's a horny toad who is selfish and demanding, with little thought for meeting our real need for intimacy.

Somewhere between our expectations and reality we make our little list of disappointments:

- "He never really talks to me."
- "I don't feel cherished."
- "There's no romance in my life anymore."
- "We never get away from all our pressures long enough to have fun together."
- "I don't remember the last time he just held me close and listened to my needs."
- "He doesn't seem to care if I enjoy our physical relationship or not. He's only interested in satisfying himself."
- "My husband has forgotten how to dream with me about the future."
- "I always thought I'd be married, but I'm not."

(Of course, not all single women long for marriage. Most singles are living fulfilling, productive, contented lives. However, to the woman who has put life on hold "waiting for Mr. Right," there can be agonizing disappointments.)

When enough of our disappointments betray our expectations, we are open to temptation in the area of sexual immorality. Our disappointments create longings for oneness the way God intended it to be. When we don't experience that oneness, the Enemy often finds a foothold.

There are many reasons Christian women give for engaging in immoral behavior. Here are some I've heard.

COMMUNICATION DIFFICULTIES

The Ladies Home Journal published a survey based on the responses of thirty thousand women. Most of them said they had chosen their mates based on sex appeal, but 80 percent said if they had to do it over again, they would choose a husband based on his ability to communicate.[1] A man who listens with compassion and carries on meaningful conversation is a great temptation to the woman who has no communication at home.

LONELINESS

This problem is especially true of a single Christian woman who has longed for marriage. In spite of a fulfilling career and close friendships, if she has a strong desire for a spouse and God closes that door, there is a sense of loss. Loneliness is just as severe for the married woman who feels cutoff from communication because her spouse is a workaholic or insensitive or lethargic. Temptation can become acute if an interesting and attractive man is available—even if he's married.

INTELLECTUAL AND/OR SPIRITUAL CHEMISTRY

This is the type of relationship that does not begin with any thought of immorality. It's usually with a business associate or someone you work closely with in a ministry situation. Since it begins as a friendship and you share common goals and a united vision for accomplishment, spending time together is a natural part of your work/ministry relationship.

The subtle nature of this "creeping immorality" is the most dangerous. It happens when two people begin working together on important projects that they feel passionate about. Psychiatrist M. Scott Peck has suggested that "spiritual and sexual desires are so closely intertwined that you cannot arouse one without arousing the other."[2]

In an editorial, Marshall Shelley, managing editor of *Leadership,* says,

> Researchers who have studied the neurochemical processes in the human brain have noted that the passion leading to spiritual fervor and the passion leading to sexual activity stem from the same kind of physiological chemistry. Though in distinct but parallel channels, spirituality and sexuality are separated by a wall thin enough for a strange osmosis to occur; the energies get mixed up.[3]

Before you get disgusted and quit reading, stay with me! I do believe there is a godly way for men and women to work in close proximity, but the spiritual and emotional levels of people are very similar. When "creative sparks" are ignited in a work or ministry situation, there can be a subliminal crossover to physical passion, often undetected at the cognitive level in the early stages.

IMMORAL LUST

This is an intense, erotic sexual urge directed at an individual, based primarily on what he looks like rather than on outstanding character or personality traits.

We normally think of men getting involved in sexual affairs for this reason; usually women need much more emotional attachment before physical intimacy occurs. However, for the woman who has been in several unsuccessful marriages and now views her fading youth and failures, there is an attitude of "Let me live for today!"

UNSPEAKABLE CIRCUMSTANCES

I mentioned that this list could go on forever. My heart goes out to the woman who is married to a man deeply involved in Internet pornography. A few of you have spouses who would just as soon get their sexual needs satisfied through masturbation rather than taking the time to meet your very real physical needs.

With tears, women who are married to homosexuals have shared their hearts with me. Some have no physical relationship with their husbands and long for physical intimacy; those who *do* have a sexual relationship often fear they will contract AIDS.

On more than a few occasions I have wept with women who know that incest is going on in their home. For a time they deny it, but then decisions must be made that are often complicated by their intense love for their spouses and their children.

Others have approached me with the honest question "My husband gets physically abusive when he drinks. At what point is it okay with God if I leave this man and marry someone who will be a good husband to me and a godly example for my children?"

Another difficult problem comes for the widowed or divorced woman who was married for years and enjoyed an active and fulfilling sexual relationship. The physical desires are still there, but she goes home to an empty bed.

God cares about our unfulfilled desires. If you are in one of these situations, God may use a variety of means to meet your needs in another way. Some possible sources for help are your pastor, a professional Christian counselor, a godly confidant, support groups, books on specialized topics, a mission of importance, or a revelation of God to you through His Word.

I know there's hope for handling our disappointments in the right way. We are able to make choices that result in actions pleasing to God when our values are firmly rooted in biblical truth.

UNANSWERED QUESTIONS

Josh McDowell and Dick Day define intimacy as:

> . . . sharing every part of our life with someone else. We all
> desire someone who will love and accept us for who we are,
> someone whom we can trust and open up to without fear of
> rejection. We desire love and intimacy, but we don't know how
> to find it.[4]

Why does it seem so difficult to develop relationships of trust? Why is a lengthy marriage the exception rather than the rule? Why do we fear rejection if we are open and vulnerable with someone else? Why are so many of our expectations of romance and physical love unfulfilled? How can we build a values system based on a godly view of intimacy the way God planned it to be?

BUILDING INTIMACY

The weekend had all of the markings of *romance*. A mystery trip. An unknown destination. Gift-wrapped packages. Anticipation built with every cleverly dropped "clue." It was the date of my twentieth wedding anniversary, and my husband had engineered a surprise. The well-kept secret turned out to be a weekend trip to Montreal, Quebec—a city we had visited on our honeymoon twenty years earlier!

After the flight, he picked up a rented Mercedes and whisked me away to our destination—an exquisite country inn along the banks of the Richelieu River. The atmosphere was perfect—an in-room jacuzzi, chocolate-covered almonds, Perrier water and lime, topped off with a lobster dinner in the prize-winning French dining room. And the croissants! Ah, the croissants and the rich, aromatic coffee followed by a dessert of fresh raspberries and blueberries smothered in maple sugar and cream. The French-speaking maitre d' and hotel clerks added to the fairy-tale experience as they turned on the charm with "Bonjour, Madame . . . et vous, Monsieur. Bon appetit!"

On this "second honeymoon," Gene and I made passionate love and reminisced a lot. With a smile I realized the weekend had begun just as I was finishing this chapter on the intense desire we have to be "held" by someone else. I asked my husband what caused a deep, abiding intimacy to grow between people. We laughed out loud as we remembered what clumsy lovers we were in the early days. Our awkward physical intimacy at that time definitely lacked skill and grace. We were quick to admit that learning how to handle our disappointments about each other in the first few years of marriage was much more important than an occasional glamorous weekend such as we were enjoying in Montreal.

We discussed the growth of relationships we have with friends and with each other. It didn't take long to establish a list of building blocks that have helped us "hold tight" to those we love.

TIME

Whether it's getting to know a person or studying someone's likes and dislikes, or helping each other through a crisis—*time* brings a bonding of oneness to a relationship. Because of the demands in our lives, the sacrifice of time is a gift that tells someone else they are valuable!

GOD

By sharing a mutual love for our Lord, His Word, and His work, we have a major "anchor point" that gives us a mutual goal, desire, and spiritual passion. If one of us (in a marriage or in a friendship) is out of close fellowship with God, our human relationship is affected. In a marriage, the sexual relationship is always affected by the spiritual relationship. Praying together and sharing spiritual truths always builds intimacy.

CONFLICT AND RESOLUTION

Every close relationship has known conflict and resolution—or no close-ness exists! Where love exists, there will be a willingness to listen, to understand, to tolerate, to confront, to forgive, to compromise, to *resolve* the distinctive "differences" we have.

TENDERNESS

Making a careful study of another person allows us to learn the art of being gentle, compassionate, and caring in a "customized" way that will best meet that person's need. Someone else senses my need for emotional or physical intimacy and meets that need in an appropriate and loving way that is perfectly suited to my one-of-a-kind personality.

"HOLDING POWER"

Tenacity might be the word to describe this part of intimacy, but it con-notes that incredible oneness that is sometimes found in marriages and/or friendships in which people support each other during physical trials, emotional distresses, spiritual upheavals, and personality explosions. It's an intimacy that "hangs in there"!

TRUST

My sexual fulfillment in marriage has a firm base in my absolute trust in Gene. He has made me feel that, apart from God, I am his all-consuming passion—his one and only partner, divinely appointed, to make his life com-plete. Sexual intimacy is a process of communicating love and affection by involving my whole person—mind, spirit, emotions, will, and body. When I present myself to Gene without embarrassment or pretense, there is a sacred kind of trust between us. I know I will not be laughed at or ridiculed. I will be held as a treasure and will know the feeling of being cherished.

The trust in a friendship, while not involving the physical intimacy of marriage, is still a bonding of mind, spirit, emotions, will, and the comfort of an appropriate godly touch, which is often expressed through a hug or a squeeze of the arm or hand. It's a way of saying, "I have confidence in your reliability and support, and I give you the same. I will 'be there' for you."

MIXED FEELINGS

In a chapter like this, I struggle with expressing in words what I feel. I believe the physical oneness of married love is an intimate communication of the whole being that is to be cherished, nurtured, and enjoyed. The building blocks for intimacy I've outlined thus far are the ideal—not a reality for very many women, including Christians! Most of my twenty years of married love have not been spent in a romantic French country inn. They've been filled with conflict and resolution, listening, sometimes giving in, sometimes "hanging tough," but always committed to a man I trust.

There are large numbers of married women who have never known physical, emotional, and spiritual intimacy with their spouses. Disappointments run deep. There are also many women who have learned the art of developing exquisite friendships that have met the need for human connection in a God-honoring way. But there are other single and married women who just want to be *heard* and *held*, and have no one meeting that need. God cares about our hunger for friendship, our sexual desires, and our spiritual needs. He created us as sexual, physical human beings, and He knows the passions and emotions that drive us.

It's never wrong to acknowledge our need. It isn't sinful to admit our powerful, driving emotional reactions. *Moi?* Tempted by sexual sin? Jealous of someone else's intimate relationships? Fantasizing about my ideal life? Yes, *moi!* By admitting our disappointments, understanding the longings they produce, and acknowledging the fierce emotions we have, we can stop long enough to run our emotions through a Bible-based set of convictions instead of being irresponsibly "driven" by our longings and hormones! If we have established godly values, our ruling passion will result in an action that is in line with a Christlike character.

Since this chapter has focused primarily on the longing for sexual fulfillment, it would be good to end with a picture of God's ideal plan for married men and women, beautifully explained in a letter written by Walter Trobish, missionary in West Africa, to a young African Christian:

My Dear Francois. . . . Let me try to tell you what it really should mean if a fellow says to a girl, "I love you." It means: "You, you, you. You alone. You shall reign in my heart. You are the one whom I have longed for; without you I am incomplete. I will give everything for you and I will give up everything for you, myself as well as all that I possess. . . . I will wait for you—it doesn't matter how long. I will always be patient with you. I will never force you, not even by words. I want to guard you, protect you and keep you from all evil. I want to share with you my thoughts, my heart and my body—all that I possess. I want to listen to what you have to say. . . . I want to remain always at your side." If you use your sexual powers apart from this kind of love, you are preparing yourself for an unhappy marriage.[5]

PART FIVE:

The Passion for Success

CHAPTER 9

I Blew It Again!:
To Transcend Failure

Failure is one of the uglies of life. We deny it,
run away from it, or upon being overtaken, fall
into permanent paralyzing fear. Probably
because of our reluctance to face it, not much
is written about the anatomy of failure.
HOWARD HENDRICKS

EXHAUSTION—PHYSICAL, emotional, and spiritual—swept over me like heavy fog in the early morning. After an intense time of ministry at a women's retreat, I flew to Detroit Metro Airport, waited for baggage, caught the van to the parking lot, and then drove the seventy miles home.

As I opened the back door, my husband greeted me with a quick hug and the news that old friends were coming through town the next day. Earlier in the day they had phoned from a vacation spot nearby and wanted to get together. The plans were made. They would meet our family at church the next morning and have Sunday dinner with us before continuing on with their trip.

I groaned, then instinctively threw visual daggers in Gene's direction and blurted out, "I love these people, but the timing of this visit couldn't be worse! Why did you invite them for dinner when you knew I was getting home from a strenuous conference at this late hour? Couldn't you have been considerate enough to suggest that tomorrow isn't a good day? How could you do this to me? Don't you have any understanding of how tired I feel after speaking all weekend? You are a creep!"

One glance at the house assured me the place needed a "touch-up" in order to properly impress the company, and I grudgingly scanned the freezer for a simple entree that could be garnished with enough flair to give me the *appearance* of a gourmet cook.

Landing in bed two hours later, I found that my mind and my body were on different frequencies. Hugging my side of the mattress so my husband would know I was intensely upset with him for putting me under this stress, I began practicing "the silent treatment," responding to his questions with grunts instead of words.

My body demanded rest, but my mind was swirling with a trio of thoughts: a review of the retreat, a plan for the next day's table arrangement for a Sunday dinner that would earn me a Betty Crocker award (and the approval and admiration of friends I *did* care about a lot), and a slow boil of ungodly thoughts toward the husband who set up the dinner I was too tired to cook! Sleep finally came, but in the morning the alarm sounded too early!

Running around like a maniac, I put the finishing touches on the house and meal. The clock was ticking and Gene was backing the car out of the garage. I called up the stairs to Jason, "Come quickly! We're already late for church!" When he emerged from his room, I couldn't believe my eyes!

With nerves already frayed by the events of the past twelve hours, I grabbed him by the shoulders, made intense, penetrating eye contact, and screamed, "How many times do I have to say it? You are not allowed to wear *white* socks with your Sunday suit and dress shoes!" My words reverberated through the hallway, suggesting an intimidating threat to anyone who might *dare* come within close proximity.

Jason's eyes filled with tears. Pulling away from me, he meekly responded, "But Mom, they were the only socks in my drawer."

Feelings of failure combined with conviction stabbed my heart. With the busyness of the past week, I had not realized the laundry wasn't done. On the surface, it appeared to be a simple misunderstanding, but his bodily posture and facial expression revealed a wounded spirit. The fierceness with which I had verbally attacked him was totally uncalled for and cruel.

Clutching him closely, I blurted out, "Honey, will you forgive me? I'm not mad at you; I'm mad at your father."

I had blown it again! Fighting back tears of my own, I paused long enough to grovel in my misery. I had just flunked another Christian maturity exam!

You're a failure, Carol Kent! The words echoed in my brain. Jason knew it. Gene knew it. I knew it. God knew it.

DEVELOPMENT OF A MONSTER AND A PRETENDER

The previous scenario changes, based on our circumstances. But married or single, we've all experienced the same situation. Combine fatigue, intense work or ministry, individuals we love, unexpected events or people, and suddenly we are magically transformed into someone we don't recognize—*a monster on the inside* (in our heart and inside the walls of our home) and *a pretender on the outside* (in front of people we want to impress)!

We often don't realize that our real problem is an insatiable passion for success. We long for people to look at us, adjust their glasses, step back, and say, "That woman knows her priorities, and no matter what the pressures of life throw at her, she has a positive attitude." When you add our Christianity to the whole package, we really believe our innate desire to transcend failure and to achieve success is based on a pure, spiritual motive. We want to demonstrate an excellent attitude and behavior that "moves on" with life—because that's what God wants us to do!

So if that's true, why am I so often a screaming monster and a skillful pretender? A quick look back at my response to unexpected company and my accompanying bad attitude gives me some painful answers:

My Expectation: After an exhausting weekend of ministry, my fondest desire was to "crash" at home. I expected to find a haven there, free from any demanding responsibilities. I planned to hug my family, brush my teeth, "hit the sack," and sleep, uninterrupted, until the next morning. I had envisioned attending the late service at my church, going out for dinner, and enjoying an afternoon of unpressured family time the next day.

My Disappointment: When I received news of the unexpected company, my expectations were destroyed. The needed rest was going to be replaced by cleaning, cooking, and "putting out the welcome mat" for guests I would love to entertain—*some other time!*

My Longing: At its roots, my longing was for an idyllic home situation, free of interruptions from the *real* world. My definition of this pastoral scene was comprised of rest, communication with my immediate family, a peaceful Sunday afternoon, and time to unwind after a stimulating, but emotionally draining, time of ministry.

My Emotions: After dreaming of my serene homecoming during the seventy-mile drive from the airport, my emotions exploded when my expectations were shattered. Putting immediate blame on my husband for orchestrating this unwanted event, I lashed into him. With mounting vocal intensity, I shouted, "You have absolutely no concept of what it feels like to work this hard all weekend and then come home to find *more* work and unwanted guests waiting for you! You think just because my job involves jetting around in an airplane and serving Jesus that it's stress-free and I can come home with almost no sleep, slap on a smile, and act like the perfect hostess in order to impress *your* friends!" (They were *my* friends, too, but my verbal abuse wouldn't have been as effective if I'd acknowledged that.)

My Belief System: At this point my emotions were quickly sifted through my "values checkpoint." In spite of a spiritually successful weekend that included several positive responses to the gospel message, my values were distorted by severe fatigue and time pressure, complicated by a consuming desire to look "successful" in front of special friends we had not seen in over a year. The following are some of the myths I subliminally believed, which contributed to a breakdown in healthy, biblical values:

- I must be a perfect hostess and a gourmet cook in order to live up to the expectations of these friends.
- I must have my house (and child) in a state of flawless order and cleanliness in order to be perceived as the wife and mother these people have always thought me to be.
- I cannot admit my physical exhaustion to the guests because it might appear that my home and ministry responsibilities are not in proper balance.
- This stress is my husband's fault, and God will hold him accountable for being so insensitive to my need for rest!

My Ruling Passion: If my convictions had been rooted in a healthy, biblical foundation, I would have been able to see the whole situation with different eyes. Instead, *I selected anger as my ruling passion*—anger directed predominately at Gene for setting me up for this extra work, and resentment taken out on Jason.

My Action: My misguided, resulting actions were twofold. First, I was a screaming monster and a silent martyr. With anger simmering, I used every opportunity to shout negative messages to the people I love the most—Gene and Jason. I chose to make Gene feel responsible for laying this burden on me. After I was "all yelled out," I assumed the "Christian" response to conflict: *the silent treatment!* My negative attitude was displayed with a disposition of rebellion, moodiness, ungodly speech, and finally withdrawal.

Second, I was a skillful pretender. After artfully engaging in silence all the way to church, I adjusted my "outer" attitude just in time to break into a warm, radiant smile as I stepped out of the car and greeted our dear friends: "Welcome to Port Huron! It's so good to see you! It's been too long! We're so glad you're here!" My act that morning could have won an Academy Award. I enthusiastically interacted with people and introduced our friends to folks in the church lobby. Faking high energy throughout the morning service and into the dinner hour that followed, I slipped into an outwardly warm relationship with Gene and Jason— and our company never guessed the rotten attitude that was behind this "snow job."

FAULTY CONVICTIONS—OUTWARD LIES AND INWARD RESENTMENT

Looking back, I wonder *why* I couldn't have lived out that scene differently. A belief system firmly rooted in truth rather than success-driven myths would have enabled me to choose a different ruling passion. In retrospect, I discovered some humbling truths.

- The friends who called were not just "passing acquaintances"; they were such a vital part of our early marriage circle of friends that if *I* had been the one answering the phone when they called, I wouldn't have considered *not* inviting them over while they were in town.
- Had I looked more closely at the house, I would have noticed that Gene had vacuumed the place from stem to stern, anticipating my late arrival.
- On closer inspection of the refrigerator, I realized that he had also gone shopping, picking out a roast, frozen vegetables, salad ingredients, rolls, and a variety of items that would make meal preparation easier at the last minute.

Instead of "seeing the good" and "believing the best," I chose the ruling passion of anger after sifting my disappointment through my distorted convictions. My faulty belief system led to outward lies (pretending everything was great in front of the guests) and inner resentment (which was demonstrated in ungodly actions directed at Gene and Jason).

Most of us are gifted at pretending life is wonderful. Instead of being honest with people about the pressures we're feeling and the failures we're experiencing, we play "make-believe," slapping on a mask instead of revealing our hearts.

Bob Benson, with hauntingly familiar words, wrote in *Come Share the Being* about how most of us "lie" when we're asked this familiar question:

"How are you?"

"GR-R-EAT! And how are you?"

"FAN-TAS-TIC! How's the work going?"

"GR-R-EAT! How about yours?"

"FAN-TAS-TIC!"

And everybody is so great and wonderful and super and colossal that you begin to wonder how anybody could possibly have taken time out for this (meeting). And that's just great if you're doing great and that's fantastic if you're really doing fantastic, but lots of times they are just words that shield and hide because it's not easy to say you're just doing lousy when everybody else is so great. . . . And I often wonder how our . . . church gatherings would turn out and how far-reaching their results would be if someone would just have the courage to say: "I'm not great—I'm not fantastic—I'm so discouraged, I'm about to die and I need your prayers and love." . . . And I wonder, too, how the world would be changed if we didn't think it was a mark of strength . . . to keep from showing our feelings.[1]

I wonder what would have happened if I had admitted to our friends that I was bone tired and a bit discouraged and too exhausted to cook. And how would they have responded if we ordered a pizza instead of having a gourmet Sunday dinner seasoned with resentment because of all the work it took to prepare? And would they have thought less of me if my house needed dusting and my son wore white socks with his Sunday suit because I hadn't done the laundry?

In all likelihood, we would have laughed and cried, admitting mutual failings in our personal and spiritual journeys, cementing an intimacy in our friendship that never could have happened in quite the same way with a "planned" visit. If my values had been healthy, I could have been honest. Instead of looking like Wonder Woman, transcending all failure, I would have been real and vulnerable and approachable. Instead, I was plastic, invincible, and "comfortably" warm while maintaining my distance.

THE HEART OF THE MATTER

I recently read the book of Matthew again and stumbled onto "The Seven Woes to the Pharisees." In the past I had always skimmed that part, wishing it was as moving as the Advent of Christ or as inspirational as the Sermon on the Mount or as exciting as the recorded miracles of Jesus. But as I read this time, I saw myself as I really am. And the whole picture made me sick! The passage is convicting:

> "I've had it with you! You're hopeless, you religion scholars,
> you Pharisees! Frauds! Your lives are roadblocks to God's
> Kingdom. . . . You're like manicured grave plots, grass clipped
> and the flowers bright, but six feet down it's all rotting bones and
> worm-eaten flesh. People look at you and think you're saints, but
> beneath the skin you're total frauds." (Matthew 23:13,27-28, MSG)

As God allowed me to see a small reflection of myself on the printed page, I noted too many similarities. In so many of my efforts to transcend failure and pursue God's excellence (with faulty values), I wind up nurturing negative attitudes, criticizing Christians who aren't like me, living by perfectionistic "lists," performing to impress others, full of hypocrisy on the inside while making "spiritual small talk" on the outside. The major difference between those Pharisees and me is that I already know God personally. I shouldn't have to play their game! But I do. And it makes me miserable.

I'm grateful that God does not have the same "performance expectations" as the Pharisees. So many times we disappoint Him, which must create a longing in His heart for the pure, unspoiled relationship He intended for us in the Garden of Eden. Instead of an emotional outburst of anger, His perfect, sinless condition leads to a ruling passion of love. And His action on our behalf?

> Meanwhile, the moment we get tired in the waiting, God's Spirit
> is right alongside helping us along. If we don't know how or
> what to pray, it doesn't matter. He does our praying in and for
> us, making prayer out of our wordless sighs, our aching groans.
> He knows us far better than we know ourselves . . . and keeps
> us present before God. That's why we can be so sure that every
> detail in our lives of love for God is worked into something
> good. (Romans 8:26-27, MSG)

That truth encourages me! As we sort through our disappointments and experience our emotional reactions, our major hope is found in Him. If we start now by ridding our lives of the false values of perfectionism and invincibility, we can build on a solid foundation, grounded in truth, and choose a ruling passion that will result in positive actions of honesty.

DON'T LOOK NOW, BUT YOUR ATTITUDE IS SHOWING!

Whether we like it or not, even without words, people can often pick up on our inner attitudes. Most of us have never thought about how we decide on the attitude of someone else, but do we have an opinion? Oh, yes! Negative attitudes are often displayed by the person who has experienced a recent failure. The disappointment is fuel for the development of the attitude.

Because we're Christians, our negative attitude isn't always displayed verbally. If we've never taken responsibility for our own ruling passions, we feel justified and wallow around in our "pity party." Somehow we feel more "Christian" if we display our displeasure with a subtle facial expression, the silent treatment, or a pre-selected bodily posture. But we're fools to think we're only showing our temporary mood or mental state. We're revealing our spiritual condition!

The stark comparison is found in Philippians 2:5-8: "Your attitude should be the same as that of Christ Jesus." In the verses that follow, we're reminded that Jesus did not consider equality with God something "to be grasped." He was made in the likeness of man and became "flesh" for us, and finally He humbled Himself and became obedient to death on the cross, creating the only bridge we have back to God.

Failure was Adam's legacy to the human race. Our failure sent Christ to the cross. But before that, our failure sent Christ to earth. I shivered as I read this description:

> How did Christmas Day feel to God? Imagine for a moment
> becoming a baby again: giving up language and muscle coordi-
> nation, and the ability to eat solid food and control your blad-
> der. God as a fetus! Or imagine yourself becoming a sea
> slug—that analogy is probably closer. On that day in
> Bethlehem, the Maker of All That Is took form as a helpless,
> dependent newborn.[2]

It's almost an unthinkable concept to envision God becoming man. One day I pondered the awful thought: What if Jesus had been so disappointed in God for making Him the sin-bearer of the world that He turned His back on our need with an "I don't care" attitude? What if? But He didn't. And because He didn't, we have the power to live by a godly set of biblical values—not in our own ability, but in His supernatural strength!

The same God who had the power to become a baby had the power to be resurrected from the dead. And that same God lives in me today! Because of Jesus' ruling passion of love, Adam's legacy of failure has been overruled.

THE PASSION TO TRANSCEND FAILURE

I hate to fail! With the messages in today's culture shouting success clichés at us, it's sometimes hard to admit our failures and human frailties to one another. I want the people around me to think I'm successful. I wish I were more spiritual than that, but we all tend to get caught up in trying to obtain favorable results that announce to the world that we've accomplished something we planned or attempted.

When we fail, there's a sense of losing power or strength. We feel somehow "insufficient," not good enough, and unsuccessful. (It's a horrible feeling to know you're trying your hardest and still doing "C+" work in a world of "A+" competitors!) When depressing thoughts of potential failure swoop down on us, we always make a choice.

Our expectations are unfulfilled, disappointment sets in, and longings are born. Emotions swing back and forth. If our Christian values are strong and vital, our ruling passion will be an attitude that is honoring to God and an ongoing action that brings Him glory. But if those values have been weakened by exhaustion, injustice, pretending, and alienation from God Himself, a negative attitude will prevail, resulting in actions that grieve the God who made us.

Someone once said, "Attitudes are the quiet judgments that shape our lives; they mold the form that living takes."

Will we experience feelings of failure again? No doubt! Will we battle with negative attitudes in the future? Chances are pretty good that next Sunday morning we'll have another opportunity to do battle with the Enemy and determine a resulting action. But in the middle of our struggle, we must remember Christmas Day!

CHAPTER 10

Self-Actualization?:
To Be All I Can Be

*If I'm not free to fail, I'm not free to take risks,
and everything in life that's worth doing
involves a willingness to take a risk and
involves the risk of failure. . . . I have to try,
but I do not have to succeed. Following
Christ has nothing to do with success
as the world sees success.*

MADELEINE L'ENGLE

WOMEN WERE stuffed everywhere in the small hotel room. My stomach hurt from laughing so hard. But beneath the laughter there were hard questions. And later, some of the women wept.

It was the midpoint of a weekend conference, and a few participants had asked if we could get together and talk about the changing roles of Christian women in today's society. I was tired, but the eager faces of these intelligent young women whetted my appetite for a challenging discussion. The topic sounded slightly controversial, and I knew it would be a lively dialogue with strong opinions being expressed.

Word spread quickly that my room would be the gathering place for this informal meeting, and the women kept coming in, sitting on the beds or cross-legged on the floor. Others dangled their legs from the dresser. I loved their informality and unpretentious manner. Most of them were youthful college graduates. Single. Married. A few were young moms. *Neat group,* I thought.

The initiators of the meeting assumed leadership. They began with a brief summary of "the changing times" for women in America, humorously dramatizing society's message to women reaching maturity in each of the following decades.

The '40s and '50s: "Be a perfect housewife and mother. Have milk and cookies ready for your children after school. Cook wonderful dinners. Support your husband's career, and have no ambitions outside your home besides the PTA and the local church."

The '60s and '70s: "Escape domestic drudgery and get a job! But more than a job, pursue a *career.* Consider postponing marriage and children for a few years. If you *do* marry, let your family be more independent."

The '80s and '90s: "You can have it all! Honey, you can bring home the bacon *and* fry it up in a pan. After your power lunch and business meetings, you can exercise at the health club and still be home in time to be a loving wife and mother. If you're a Christian, God and church need to be in this picture too—somewhere near the top—*but you're a 'woman of the '90s' and you are the image of success!*"

The New Millennium: "Women can't have it all. Time demands are building on every front—family, career, civic, and church responsibilities. To be worth a woman's time, a meeting has to have 'take-home value.' With the threat of terrorism, she has new fears for the future of her children."

Suddenly the mood in the room changed drastically and the women got very serious. The unplanned, spontaneous way this group had come together, combined with the relaxation of laughter, sparked peak-level communication and bottom-line honesty. One by one these young women began voicing their various frustrations and questions. Hard questions. Deep frustrations.

- "I'm thirty-two years old and I'm still trying to figure out what I want to *be* when I grow up! Being single doesn't allow me the buffer of another person helping with household expenses while I investigate other job opportunities. I long to be in a work or ministry situation that will allow me to fully develop my potential. My deepest desire is to be all that I can be. I know I have potential that hasn't been tapped yet. I'm locked in a dead-end job because I'm afraid to risk failure—and bankruptcy! What should I do?"

- "I'm afraid of the word *average.* My mother and my older sisters live from one day to the next without any visible thought or planning. My worst fear is that I'll get to be old without having reached my greatest potential. I don't have to be *famous* to feel fulfilled, *but I do want to reach beyond the ordinary and excel at something.* Is that unspiritual?"

- "I just passed the bar exam this year. My parents sacrificed to put me through undergraduate school and then law school. My husband has a good job—nothing close to my earning potential—but his employment *does* meet our basic living expenses and a little more. Now that I'm the mother of two small children, becoming a practicing attorney has lost its appeal. I believe there's nothing more important I could do right now than be with my kids, but I'm feeling tremendous pressure because of my parents' expectations. They can't understand why I would consider *wasting* all of that time and money on my education if I'm not going to *use* it. Are my desires wrong?"

- "My engagement was announced last week, and in three months I'll be married to a seminary student. My degree is in business administration, and I'm planning a career in marketing and sales. I think I can be a pastor's wife *and* a businesswoman, but I keep running into people who are shocked with that thought. I know several pastors' wives who are teachers or nurses, but the thought of a pastor's wife in business seems to scare people. Why shouldn't I be allowed to pursue what I'm best at without struggling under the expectations of individuals who define the role of the pastor's wife differently than I do? This makes me so angry!"

- "I feel trapped. I married at eighteen, had four children by the time I was twenty-five, and have never had an opportunity to go to college. Whenever I'm with a group of women like you, I feel inadequate. One of my earliest memories dates back to third grade when I gave an incorrect answer to the teacher's question, and in front of the whole class she said, 'Why can't you be as good a student as your sister was?' It seems like I've always felt inferior. It usually terrifies me to be with educated people, but I want to change. What can I do?"

- "Prestige and power are not all that important to me, but I *do* have a longing to know if I'm living up to the potential that God placed in me. I've been a secretary in a downtown office for the last four years, but I've been experiencing 'creative restlessness.' Is there something else I should be doing with my life? How do I know if God wants me to be content where I am, or if He wants me to step out in a new direction, even if it feels risky?"

UNFULFILLED EXPECTATIONS

These women were voicing serious questions. And I didn't have answers. But I sure did identify with them! Disappointments had given birth to longings, and emotions were being felt and expressed. Most of the women were just beginning to run those disappointments through their values and convictions. They had not yet decided on a ruling passion and a resulting action, but they were longing for a sense of direction.

I mentally ran through their list of disappointments:

- Desiring to try different employment, but being held back by economic limitations and fear of failure
- Hoping to do something extraordinary with time and talents, but feeling "average"
- Longing for parents to accept a personal choice to be "self-actualized" at home, but being disappointed by their negative response
- Wanting Christians to understand the compatibility of a business career and the role as a pastor's wife, but feeling rejected and judged
- Wishing for educational opportunities and the resulting self-esteem, but being held back by the constraints of time, responsibilities, and fear
- Expecting to be in a fulfilling job, but feeling unchallenged and a bit unspiritual for being restless

SELF-ACTUALIZATION?

How in the world are we supposed to combine our Christianity and our deep desire to be fully the women God created us to be? If I'm honest, I know I have a longing to discover who the real "me" is. Most of us wonder if we're working at what we're best at or if we should be exploring other possibilities.

We long to have answers to key questions:

- What are my greatest assets?
- What are my personal limitations?
- How can I be most effective as a woman in my sphere of influence?·
- If I'm comfortable with my choices, should I worry about the disapproval of other people?

Even as we review these questions, we wonder: Is this kind of thinking too self-centered? Maybe God wants us to deny those thoughts and feelings and have more "spiritual" aspirations.

A VIVID MEMORY

Monday through Friday my life was always the same. Blackboard. Data projector. Students. Teachers' lounge. Lesson plans. *I was sick of it!* And I felt guilty for being sick of it.

Four years earlier I was so full of expectations and anticipation. I had just received my bachelor of science degree in speech education. I was going to be the best English and speech teacher that ever hit Fremont Junior High School! Students were going to enjoy my classes, and I knew they would fall in love with nouns, verbs, gerunds, and participles. All they needed was an enthusiastic, well-prepared teacher and the right motivation.

I had it all figured out. The public school classroom was going to be my arena for being "salt" in the real world. The teaching would be educationally excellent—but students would be drawn to the Lord as a result of being in my classes. It was my opportunity to be a Christian woman of influence in my chosen profession.

Now, just four years later, I was a restless clock-watcher who secretly wished I'd majored in something other than education. My students honored me by voting me "Teacher of the Year"! On the surface I looked successful. *Why was I so discontent?*

ANALYZING OUR PASSION FOR SUCCESS

We all have a desire to transform from an "average" woman into an "extraordinary" woman. We're curious to know what our potential really is. Inside we long *to know who we are* and *to be our truest self.* Success, for most of us, is more than accomplishing something we planned or attempted. It's finding our unique niche in this world and then fulfilling our goals with all our might. We long to feel great about the results and to have the affirmation of significant people. Without that approval—from ourselves and others—we often don't *feel* successful.

In a sense, the women who gathered in my hotel room the night of the weekend conference were expressing the same disappointment I was feeling after four years of teaching. In spite of our different stages of life, we had much in common.

Our Expectation: If we were Christians at the time we approached adulthood, most of us believed that, with God's help, we would make a decision on a career or vocation that would make us happy and fulfilled for a lifetime. We knew we should pray hard, keep our eyes open for divine guidance, and then act. We expected the result to be personal fulfillment in a life situation that allowed us to live up to our greatest potential. When I signed my first teaching contract, I *knew* my expectation would be met.

Our Disappointment: For many of us, disappointment comes over a period of time. I was surprised that my fourth year of teaching wasn't as fulfilling as the first few years. With all the time and money spent on my education, combined with my desire to make a spiritual difference in the lives of my students, I was disappointed in myself for being discontented.

Our Longing: At the root level, our deepest longing is for "the absence of restlessness," to be satisfied with God's purpose for our lives. On the surface, our longing is for self-actualization—not putting ourselves forward, but finding out that which we do best. We long to discover the all-satisfying, custom-made spot to showcase our God-given talents in a way that will bring personal and spiritual fulfillment.

Our Emotions: At this point our emotions go wild! I walked into my empty classroom one day, closed the door, surveyed the room, and shouted: *"If I am still in this schoolroom doing the same thing twenty-five* *years from now, I will go crazy!"* On my knees a few days later, I prayed, "Lord, I love my students. I know You've used me in a unique way to reach several kids in this school for Christ. I do not understand my current frustration. I feel like You've designed me to do something else. I hate myself for not being satisfied with the job I already have! *Please help me!"*

Our Belief System: Fortunately, we have a "convictions clearinghouse" that will always help us to make a decision on our ruling passion. In our hearts we know that God has gifted us and that we're created in His image with incredible potential to do something extraordinary with our lives. If those convictions are built on biblical truth, the end result will honor God. But sometimes those convictions are damaged by life's negative events and disillusionment with God. More often, the problem is our own faulty thinking. Some of the myths we accept as truth are these:

- I am only as good as my job description.
- Because I'm a Christian, God will always make me happy in my work.
- If other people don't approve of my choices, I must be wrong.
- God will love me more if I'm "above average."
- If I got poor grades as a kid, I'm unintelligent.
- If I try something new and fail, I'm out of God's will.
- Feeling creative restlessness in my work means I'm discontented with God.

Our Ruling Passion: Our ruling passion will always determine our action. After searching my heart and feeling a tremendous struggle within, my ruling passion was determined. I would practice contentment in my job situation, not based on my feelings (which were negative), but based on my trust in God (the same God I had trusted in the past when I *agreed* with His leading).

Our Action: It was true for most of the women gathered in the hotel room that their action had not yet been determined. My action was to *wait* (with my eyes open), while practicing contentment.

WAITING—WITH IMPATIENCE

Waiting rooms. I don't like them. Someone else has power over my carefully planned schedule for the day. And do they care? Of course not! If they did, they wouldn't overschedule like they do. Right?

And sometimes when I'm sitting around waiting for God's direction and no opportunity manifests itself, I'm disappointed. On the surface it seems like He doesn't care. Everything seems "status quo." Boring. Nothing exciting on the horizon.

Last week I punched the television remote control button and flipped on a cable program. The advertisement on the screen was promoting a videotape I could order for $19.95. The title made me laugh out loud—"Play the Piano Overnight!" The commercial featured the testimonial of a celebrity and demonstrations of people who claimed to have used this "secret formula" to master the keyboard in one day. I was tempted to call my mother to tell her she had wasted hundreds of dollars on piano lessons, to say nothing of my own wasted hours of agonizing practice through the years. *Why didn't somebody tell me there was a way to avoid waiting?* (The advertisement wasn't on this week. Maybe the Better Business Bureau caught up with them! Could it be that there's no *real* way to avoid waiting for some things?)

WAITING—WITH EXPECTANT HOPE

As a child I had memorized Isaiah 40:31 (KJV):

But they that wait upon the LORD shall renew their strength; they shall mount up with wings as eagles; they shall run, and not be weary; and they shall walk, and not faint.

One day while reading the same verse in the NIV translation, I made a wonderful discovery. It began, "But those who hope in the LORD will renew their strength. They will soar on wings like eagles." That was the answer for which I had been looking. For the Christian, "waiting" is not the opposite of progress or the barrier to success. Waiting is *expectant hope.*

God created us with an overwhelming desire to *soar.* Our desire to develop and use every ounce of potential He's placed in us is not egotistical. He designed us to be tremendously productive and "to mount up with wings like eagles," realistically dreaming of what He can do with our potential.

The next day my son was going to the library, and I asked him to bring home a book on eagles. I chuckled when he came through the door with an elementary reader, written on the fourth-grade level, titled *Raccoons and Eagles.* But my amusement soon turned to fascination as I studied the process involved in soaring:

> The eagle's bones are hollow and its entire skeleton weighs only half as much as its approximately 7,000 feathers. The 15-pound weight of the bird along with its huge wingspan of six or seven feet makes it hard to get up in the air in its own strength.
>
> But the weight that makes an eagle clumsy on the ground will, in the air, give it the stability and lift needed for prolonged soaring and gliding. An eagle's bulk makes flapping flight hard work, so she finds a strong updraft (a wind deflected upward by a hillside), spreads her broad, flat wings, and rides, carried by the power of something other than herself. The eagle is able to soar effortlessly for hours on these rising "thermals," without ever flapping its wings.[1]

So many times in our lives we hold back from trying something new because of fear of failure. In our hearts, we long to soar, but then we think about the practical side of things. What about the constraints of time, money, responsibilities, and other people's negative opinions about what we're attempting? Yet, in a corner of our truest self, there's an eagle waiting for a rising thermal, looking for the courage to spread those wings, and scared to death of failing. So instead of soaring, held up by the power of the Almighty, we stay close to the ground, hoping to move more quickly from one task to the next with "flapping flight."

FLAWED BELIEFS PRODUCE FLAPPING FLIGHT

The myths we looked at earlier remind us of the subtle way the Enemy "clips our wings" and keeps us grounded. As the retreat participants in that hotel room communicated their frustrations and fears of trying "to become all they could be," I realized they were battling the same problem I still struggle with—distorted convictions that sound like truth when we are not immersed in the Word of God.

Psychiatrist M. Scott Peck gives an analogy that helped me understand the dangers of believing these untruths:

> Our view of reality is like a map. . . . If the map is true and accurate, we will generally know where we are, and if we have decided where we want to go, we will generally know how to get there. If the map is false and inaccurate, we generally will be lost.[2]

Our only hope for having an accurate map is to study the Bible. Knowledge of the truth will strengthen our convictions. Dr. Chris Thurman, in *The Lies We Believe,* says:

> The Bible is God's primary way of giving us the most important truths we need to fight our lies. It's no coincidence that Satan was called the "father of lies." . . . To the degree we choose

truth, we'll react appropriately to what happens to us and experience a peace which transcends all understanding. To the degree we choose lies, we will be emotionally and spiritually miserable. When it's a mixture, as it usually is, we live with mixed emotional and spiritual signals.[3]

The lies keep us in bondage and hold us back from being true to ourselves and to God. When we rewrite those lies with biblical truth, instead of "flapping flight," we can choose to soar. Soaring isn't always fun. There's danger and risk—and when you're a beginner, there's more fear than there is later. But there's also exhilaration, freedom, fulfillment, and a sense of being "carried" by a Power beyond yourself.

EAGLE FLIGHT TRAINING

The story of Esther has always intrigued me. Orphaned. Raised by a relative. Beautiful. Pursued. One year of beauty treatments—special oils, perfumes, and cosmetics—to make a good first impression. Open to wise counsel. Crowned "Queen" Esther by King Xerxes.

What more excitement could a story have? When I was much younger, I envisioned Esther as the "Barbie doll" and King Xerxes as the "Ken doll." I realize the analogy is hard to imagine, but I'm a visual thinker, and it was thrilling to put myself in Barbie's place the day she was "picked" by King Xerxes (Ken) to be the queen. In my youthful romanticism I wondered how a woman could want to soar any higher than that.

But these were troubled times for the Jews, and their lives were in danger. Word came to Esther from Mordecai: "If you remain silent at this time, relief and deliverance for the Jews will arise from another place, but you and your father's family will perish. And who knows but that you have come to royal position for such a time as this?" (Esther 4:14).

Esther was face-to-face with the biggest risk of her life. God had placed the potential in her to gain an audience with the king. It meant uncertainty, possible failure, and fear. Talk about "eagle" flight training! The rest is history. Because of her obedience and willingness to transcend the fear of failure, her Jewish people were saved from possible annihilation at this frightening time in their history.

IF ONLY I COULD BE AN EAGLE

When I read about women like that, I feel discouraged looking at myself. I have never saved a whole race of people from being wiped out. But I am a woman, and I, like Esther, have a deep desire to be transformed from an ordinary woman into an extraordinary woman who is reaching my potential in all areas.

Several years ago, when my expectations of enjoying teaching junior high students were unfulfilled, I longed to be doing something else. Emotions raged and my *daily choice* was between contentment and dissatisfaction. When my ruling passion was contentment, I was able to choose the action of waiting—with my eyes open!

My biggest battle during this time was to rewrite one of my myths and change it to the truth: "Feeling creative restlessness in my work *does not* mean I'm discontented with God." One of the most helpful activities for me during this time of biblical reprogramming was to honestly and prayerfully answer several questions—first on paper, then face-to-face with a friend.

- What causes most of my frustration, anxiety, and pressure?
- What produces most of my fun, pleasure, and enjoyment?
- Why am I doing the job I'm doing? (If it's only for the money, that's not good enough!)
- What really motivates me?
- What is the most meaningful compliment I've ever received?
- If I could do anything I wanted, without the restrictions of time,

money, education, or current responsibilities, what would it be?

- What do I want to be doing ten years from now?
- What do I want on my gravestone?
- What are my greatest strengths?
- What women (currently living) do I admire most?

As I reviewed the answers to those questions, God repeatedly brought to mind the Scripture I had selected as my life's verse: "Thou wilt shew me the path of life: in thy presence is fulness of joy; at thy right hand there are pleasures for evermore" (Psalm 16:11, KJV).

The "creative restlessness" in my heart was God's way of preparing me to risk something new. The process of becoming "who I am" is ongoing. Since those early days of struggle in a junior high classroom, it has included motherhood, teaching pregnant girls, becoming a director of women's ministries in a local church, being a teacher for an international Bible study organization, launching out into public speaking, and then training others in communication skills and developing Speak Up Speaker Services. Right now my greatest risk is writing. Is this God's next opportunity for me to stretch beyond my comfort zone? What if I fail?

We all have days of "flapping flight" as we struggle to find our customized, God-ordained niche. And just when we think we've found it, He gives us a glimpse of another challenge. Will we stay in "the comfort zone" or will we move into "the risk zone"? More than a few times I have failed, "flapped," and tried again. With each success comes greater confidence. And one day when we spread our wings in the updraft, being lifted by the thermal of His unwavering strength, the whole process will seem normal. Soaring and gliding—that's what we were designed for—not free of risks, not removed from all failure (we still live in this fallen world!), but soaring with a new sense of trust and an inner burst of freedom.

Our desire "to be all we can be" is from God. It is not essential that other people validate our success. It's encouraging when they do, but it is not what's ultimately important. When we walk in obedience and fix our minds on truth, our disappointments will eventually produce ruling passions that will result in actions that are honorable and holy. That's when we soar on wings like eagles!

PART SIX:

The Passion for Spirituality

CHAPTER 11

Whatever the Abundant Life Is, I Want It!: To Be a Confident, Growing Christian

*What makes life worthwhile is having a big
enough objective, something which catches our
imagination and lays hold of our allegiance;
and this the Christian has, in a way that
no other man has. For what higher, more
exalted, and more compelling goal can
there be than to know God?*

J. I. PACKER

J ULIE WAS breathless with excitement. The women's retreat had been nothing short of spectacular! The music was perfect—sometimes upbeat, sometimes reflective. And the speakers gave such inspiring messages! Julie had come to know Christ as her personal Savior as a child, but she knew this weekend would be life-changing for her. The time away had been a little touch of heaven. Now she was headed home, ready to impact her world for Christ!

As Julie's car rounded the corner, she got a glimpse of the house. Home sweet home! She couldn't wait to tell the family about her uplifting experience at the retreat. As she burst into the house, the dog ran smack-dab into her legs, knocking her off balance. Upon impact, Julie's overnight bag flew off in one direction while her Bible landed in the dog dish. At that moment Jennifer, her six-year-old, rushed into the room screaming, "Mom, David's been picking on me and Dad won't stop him. I hate David and I'm mad at Daddy!"

The television was blaring from the family room and her husband hollered, "Glad you're home, Julie. I'll talk to you after the game's over. Oh, I almost forgot. Your mother called. She's coming for a few days. Said she'd be here for dinner tonight."

Disturbing music bellowed from David's room upstairs. Still in a prone position after colliding with the dog, Julie surveyed the remnants of her kitchen. Dishes were piled high in the sink and randomly placed all over the countertop. A trail of popcorn ran from the microwave oven to the television set. Pop bottles and candy wrappers were here and there. Lifting herself from the floor, she stood up and tried to take a step. Her feet were mobile, but her shoes weren't. Pancake syrup had glued them to the floor.

With blood pressure rising, Julie stomped down the hall, crushing every kernel of popcorn in her path. Finally arriving at the throne of King Couch Potato, she sucked in air, took careful aim, and fired: "I am mad. No, I'm not mad. *I'm furious! I leave for one weekend—just one weekend—and this place turns into a garbage dump!* There's garbage in the kitchen. Garbage on the floor. Garbage sports on the television. Garbage music on the radio in your son's room. And Jennifer has had no supervision. This place could not be in worse shape if I'd left the dog in charge! And you call yourself a father?"

Bull'seye! Her ammunition was gone, but Julie knew she hit her mark. Pivoting on her heel, she stiffened and marched out of the room like a trained soldier leaving the battlefield. Enemy wounded. Mission accomplished.

Now back in the kitchen, she picked up her overnight bag and then reached for her Bible. Wiping dog food off the gilded edges, she started to crumble. There was a knot in her throat. The tough lady was beginning to fight back tears. The in-charge, always-under-control, Mrs. I-Am-All-Together was falling apart.

Pondering the "life-changing" commitment she made on the weekend, Julie voiced her question out loud: "God, where are You now? Is it possible for a woman to experience true spirituality in the real world? How can I be a confident, growing Christian with a family like mine? Every time I think I have it together, I don't. Every time I get spiritually inspired, my life falls apart. My emotions are exploding. I'm worried about my kids. I don't understand my husband. My faith in God is like a roller coaster. When I'm at the top, I can conquer the world and Jesus is wonderful. When I'm at the bottom, I feel like giving up. Why doesn't somebody write a for-real book called 'Dog Dish Christianity: How to Live the Abundant Life with a Rotten Husband and Crummy Kids'?"

"READY? AIM! FIRE!"

What really happens to us when we have days like Julie experienced? Married or single, we all have circumstances, events, and people who shoot holes in our spiritual balloon. When the helium is fresh, the balloon reaches ever upward, cavorting with the wind, resisting the downward tug of the string, bouncing back up to full grandeur with every playful pull.

But within a short time, the gas that pumped it up begins to escape. The balloon loses some of its elasticity and begins its downward spiral, sometimes lingering, wistfully trying to imitate its former status, but falling far short of the goal. Suddenly it's Monday morning and the exhilarating retreat weekend has now been replaced by the daily grind. Does Christianity work without a background of inspirational music and motivational speakers?

THE PASSION FOR SPIRITUALITY

The abundant Christian life. I want it. You want it. Some people seem to have it. But *how* do we get it? Remember the verse that says, "1 am come that they might have life, and that they might have it more abundantly" (John 10:10, KJV)? Evidently there *is* a way to get it, and that's *why* Jesus came in the first place, but probably the people who experience the "abundant" Christian life have husbands and kids who are more spiritual than ours. Or maybe single women are the only ones who get to experience Christianity at its best. Wrong!

The phrase "abundant Christian life" seems to indicate there's a way to live out our spirituality with confidence, fruitfulness, and increasing maturity. But with all due respect for the countless theologians who've written on this topic, I still need help with knowing how all the rhetoric applies to the real world. With an IQ like mine (something less than genius level!), I need somebody to spell it out. *How* can I live the Christian life abundantly in the framework of my daily life?

BLUEPRINT OF THE WAR ZONE

As we take a look back at Julie's situation, we may gain some insights that will help us.

Julie's Expectation: After her uplifting spiritual retreat weekend, Julie was bursting with enthusiasm for the Lord. She *had* to tell her precious family about the messages, the music, and the new closeness she experienced in her walk with God. Her expectations were threefold:

1. She wanted the family to vicariously experience the spiritual mountaintop of the weekend.
2. She expected her husband to get his heart right with God and become the spiritual leader of the home after he listened to the

CD of the female speaker she had just heard at the retreat. Even though she knew that he didn't like "women preachers," she was sure that this woman's message would "nail" him and he would come back to God.

3. She anticipated coming home to a clean, well-run household with a happy husband and children. She envisioned Jennifer and David participating in games and outdoor activities with their father, enjoying the closeness of family ties and cherishing time alone with Dad.

Julie's Disappointment: Her devastation was so obvious we almost don't need to comment on it. The family did not care at all about reviewing *her* spiritual high. The *last* thing her husband wanted to listen to was "that lady preacher's CD," nor was his heart any closer to coming back to the Lord. And as for the house, we've already said enough! And how about the close family time? Talk about disappointments! She had them!

Julie's Longing: At best, Julie's deepest desire was for a little hunk of Eden in her own backyard. She wanted her marriage and family life to be the way God intended it before sin corrupted the human race. With her own heart touched supernaturally on the weekend, she believed God could, and that He *would,* touch those in her family, too. She longed for a family that lived out the principles of the abundant Christian life. With an honest heart, she knew her goal was to be a confident, growing Christian, and she wanted the same for her husband and children. If Julie couldn't have that, she at least felt she deserved a clean home and a civil family. Disappointment "lowered the boom," and Julie's longing produced flat-out rage!

Julie's Emotions: To say that Julie "blew a gasket" would be an understatement. It was as if she shook up a bottle of soda pop, positioned it in front of her husband, and "pulled the cork"! Julie's emotional outburst even surprised *her!* She got so involved in her "garbage" speech that she worked in a line from previous disappointments as she referred to his "garbage sports on television."

Julie's Belief System: Julie had just experienced a dynamic, encouraging conference centered on biblical principles for successful Christian living. At first glance it would appear that her belief system could not have been any stronger than it was after the uplifting weekend retreat. The problem for Julie was that she lived her Christian life from one "high" to the next. She seldom opened her Bible in between Sundays. The mainstays of her prayer life consisted of asking God to bless the food and begging Him to get through to her unspiritual husband and son.

In spite of her emotionally charged decision made at the retreat to "set her world on fire for Jesus," she still had damaged convictions due to her misconceptions about the Christian life and her lack of time in the Word of God. If Julie's belief system had been based on truth instead of misconceptions, she could have made a godly decision, with or without the emotional high of the women's retreat.

Julie's Ruling Passion: Sifting her strong emotions through a false set of values, she chose ruling passions of resentment and anger.

Julie's Action: With resentment still steaming, her destructive actions varied from screaming to silence. First, the anger was directed toward her husband for being so lethargic and uninvolved with the children. One of her favorite actions was to play her CDs of Christian messages and music loudly when he was home. She wanted to let him know he was *not* the spiritual leader she wanted him to be and he should feel guilty about it. Her anger also had a ripple effect on the children as they got caught in the wake of their parents' war zone.

Finally, the anger was directed toward God—subliminally at first, then blatantly. After all, the God of creation, Mighty Worker of miracles, *could* get through to her husband if He wanted to. Couldn't He? Then why didn't He? If Julie's values had been biblical, she could have lived her life by the principle we read in 1 Peter 3:1-2 (MSG): "Be good wives to your husbands, responsive to their needs. There are husbands who, indifferent as they are to any words about God, will be captivated by your life of holy beauty."

IDENTIFYING THE BATTLEGROUND

Julie's unfulfilled expectations brought about deep disappointment. In her heart, she longed to be a growing Christian, confident in her walk with God. Instead, she felt like a spiritual zero, aimlessly looking for a quick-fix solution and wondering what to do next. The flaws in her belief system produced confusion, and the confusion made her question her own faith.

It happens to all of us at one time or another. A missionary writes about the fruit of faulty foundations:

> Our inability to develop a truly God-shaped set of expectations
> easily could leave us wandering out the forty years or so of our
> adult lives in our own self-made desert wilderness. In my case,
> the greatest consequence of long-term, misplaced expectations
> has been their deadening effect on spiritual vitality. I questioned
> God, myself, my circumstances. . . . *God must not love me the*
> *way He loves others,* I thought. *I must be on Jesus' blacklist. I*
> *guess I'm just one of those Christians that God can't use.*[1]

Our greatest battles most often come when we get caught up in the comparison game. Most of us right now could name somebody we think "has it together" spiritually. And what's her profile?

She looks good. She sounds good. She smells good. And her baby never spits up on anyone. This woman's children don't talk out loud during church services. Her cat uses the litter box. She is a wonderful Bible teacher, and she knows all the appropriate Scripture verses (from memory) for everybody's need. She's always smiling and never yells. This woman has never had a run in her stockings. Her husband is a spiritual giant, and when she teaches Bible study she always makes reference to his strong Christian leadership in their home. She leads such a "blessed" life, it appears that God loves her more than He loves you.

We hate her. (We know we shouldn't use that word about a "dear" Christian sister, but it is our honest emotional response.)

If I pause long enough to think rationally, I know the battleground is my own mind. I have a powerful ability to visualize what isn't real. The dictionary defines *imagination* as "the act or power of forming a mental image of something not present to the senses or never before wholly perceived in reality." When I think about how "spiritually perfect" someone else's life is, my imagination always makes her life better than it is and it makes my life worse than it really is. In my mind, she is "dripping" with the fruits of the Spirit, and I can't even find a blossom on my fruit tree!

As I create untrue mental images, the Enemy attacks with vengeance. Satan has had years to observe me, and he knows me better than I know myself. He has already determined my point of vulnerability—the mind! Ephesians 6:12 (MSG) confirms that there's a war raging: "This is no afternoon athletic contest that we'll walk away from and forget about in a couple of hours. This is for keeps, a life-or-death fight to the finish against the Devil and all his angels."

Is there any hope of defeating the "Father of Lies"?

RECOGNIZING MISCONCEPTIONS

In our quest to establish healthy values, we need to stop long enough to analyze our thinking. Why do we act and react the way we do?

When we own up to the truth, we realize we choose our own ruling passions, based on the state of our minds at the time of decision making. Second Corinthians 10:5 (MSG) says, "We use our powerful God-tools for smashing warped philosophies, tearing down barriers erected against the truth of God, fitting every loose thought and emotion and impulse into the structure of life shaped by Christ."

My ungodly imaginations produce misconceptions about the Christian life. I don't like to admit it, because I'm made responsible to God for replacing my thoughts with biblical truth that will produce sound values. I would prefer to have Him supernaturally "zap" me with right thinking. Instead, He's given me His Word as a guidebook. Void of excuses for blaming other people and events for "doing me in," I must face the truth: If my convictions are based on unbiblical misconceptions, it's my fault when I act and react with ungodly responses.

In the opening story, Julie's misconceptions were typical of the flawed values of all of us who've failed at being confident, growing Christians. Add to that our response to "Mrs. Perfect and Her Happy Christian Family," and it's easy to itemize the list of misconceptions that subtly get ingrained in our values.

- God can't use me unless I'm a spiritual giant.
- If I work hard, God will give me spiritual fruit in my ministry.
- It's my Christian duty to be perfect.
- Visible results are the measuring stick of spiritual effectiveness.
- I could do more for God if my family were perfect and I were more talented.
- The abundant Christian life is always filled with adrenaline-producing highs.
- I would be a better Christian if my husband loved Jesus more. (We can substitute mother, sister, brother, or friend for the word *husband*.)

REALITY STRATEGY

For me, facing reality starts with comparing my misconceptions with what the Bible actually says. I've always claimed for myself that inspiring passage from Jeremiah 17:7-8:

> Blessed is the man who trusts in the LORD, whose confidence is
> in him. He will be like a tree planted by the water that sends
> out its roots by the stream. It does not fear when heat comes; its
> leaves are always green. It has no worries in a year of drought
> and never fails to bear fruit.

On first glance it appears that if I work hard for God, I will always
bear spiritual fruit. Wrong! Working hard is *not* what it takes to be a fruitful Christian.

My whole personality rebels against that fact! I *love* to work and be
rewarded for it. On those fancy psychological tests, my profile comes out
as the person who likes work before play. I like to know what God's "to-
do" list has on it for me each day. Then I like to perform with excellence
(faithfully checking off each item on my list as I come to it), and at the
end of the day I'd like to be rewarded with the prize fruit mentioned in
Galatians 5:22: "love, joy, peace, patience, kindness, goodness, faithfulness, gentleness and self-control."

The unbiblical view that hard work always results in spiritual fruit
leaves no room for God-ordained interruptions, health problems, waiting
rooms, or people who think or speak more slowly than I do. And the very
nature of patience (idling your motor when you feel like stripping your
gears) is *flexibility* instead of *rigidity*.

Last week I met with a group of Christian professional women, and
when a psychologist looked at my scores on a test we had taken, she said,
"Do you know you have the most *intense* personality type there is?" (No
surprise there!) My unbendable work ethic turns me into a screaming wife
and mother (like Julie) one minute and a basket case of tears the next.
How can I ever be a fruitful Christian by biblical standards when I'm
trapped in this "structured" mind-set?

My *expectation* is to be a woman who trusts in the Lord and brings glory to Him. The *disappointment* comes when my rigid work ethic doesn't bring the fulfillment of true spirituality. My *longing* is to experience the fruit of the Spirit by reacting to life's events (including the surprises) with love, joy, peace, patience, kindness, goodness, faithfulness, gentleness, and self-control.

When that doesn't happen, my *emotions* take over, and I try "to organize this place or person or project (whatever is in my path) into shape!" If I'm working with a non-family member, my emotions are like water behind a dam—at times turbulent and powerful, but with the outward "appearance of control." If I'm with family or close friends, the dam breaks, flooding the person with negative criticism and undeserved verbal attacks.

My next step involves running those emotions through my *belief system*. Accepting the misconception "If I work hard, God will give me spiritual fruit in my ministry," I decide on a *ruling passion* of zealous workaholism. And my resulting *action* is to control everything and everybody in my path, manipulating them into doing (my opinion of) God's will. And in my heart I think I'm doing something good for God and them. But I'm not.

"Reality strategy" means taking a closer look at *the tree planted by the water.* It must be important because the Bible refers to it in Psalm 1:3-4 as well as in Jeremiah 17:7-8. Since God doesn't waste words, He must have wanted us to capture the essence of this "tree theology."

When our firm belief, assurance, and trust are in Him, we are "like a tree . . . that sends out its roots by the stream." Instead of experiencing outward anxiety and attitudes of workaholism, perfectionism, and manipulation of others, we spend time establishing the inside root system. We do this through prayer, Bible study, discipline, listening without talking, meditating, memorizing His Word, evaluating our motives before organizing activities— *being* rather than *doing.* The reward is not applause from an audience. No standing ovations here. The quiet results are twofold: *invisible* (no fear when the "heat" is on) and *visible* ("green leaves in drought time").

A spiritual renewal. I need to experience this. No music. No speakers. Just Him and me. I think I'm hungry for it. But I'm afraid of it. I'm more used to noise. Silence frightens me. It means having to face my true motives, revealing my hidden heartbeat. It means owning up to my *real* reasons for working so hard and admitting I'm a beginner at prayer even though I've known Him personally for years. It means reading His Word because I long to hear from Him rather than to mark my progress on the "Read Through the Bible in a Year" chart. It means discovering my true "hidden agenda" and dumping my calendar and lists for a block of time with no telephone, no Internet, no radio, no television, no outside interference, and no deadlines.

I wonder what it was like for Moses to enter the Tent of Meeting. It must have been humbling and spectacular, for "The LORD would speak to Moses face to face, as a man speaks with his friend" (Exodus 33:11). I'm really wondering what He wants to say to me—if only I'd give Him a chance.

PROFILE OF A COMMITTED SOLDIER

Apart from Christ, nowhere in Scripture do we see a more passionate man than Paul. I'm sure he could identify with workaholics. Before his conversion, he persecuted the saints with full gusto. After his Damascus Road experience, he used that same intense drive to serve His God with equal zeal.

On his second missionary journey he and Silas had several "waits" before they were led by the Spirit—in a very roundabout way—to go to Philippi. (I like the direct route myself, and I have a feeling Paul felt the same way.) I wonder what his *expectations* were. A city-wide evangelistic crusade? Media coverage? An equipping seminar for local pastors? An autograph party at the local Christian bookstore? (Oops! I guess his books weren't off the press yet.)

We would no doubt be safe in assuming there were some *disappointments* upon arrival. Instead of an impressive crowd to share with, they met a handful of women by a river and shared their faith. One responded. Then a slave girl followed them. Paul cast a demon out of her in Jesus' name, thus destroying the earning potential of the girl's owners. The rest is history. Paul and Silas were jailed, stripped, and severely beaten, with their feet fastened in stocks.

If I had been there, my deepest longing would have been to escape and leave! Not Paul. His *longing* was a deep yearning to preach the gospel and lead people to Jesus Christ. Paul's *emotion,* when defined as an initial automatic response, is unclear. There is nothing in Acts 16 that would lead us to believe he was upset by this outrageous treatment. Paul's *belief system* was so rooted in a God-honoring foundation that his *ruling passion* of choosing joy in spite of suffering was almost automatic. He practiced the presence of Christ. Thus, his *action* of praying and singing hymns to God in the middle of his imprisonment led to another holy action. Instead of escaping after the earthquake, he stayed and led the jailer to Christ.

It was Paul who gave this challenge: "Endure hardship with us like a good soldier of Christ Jesus. No one serving as a soldier gets involved in civilian affairs—he wants to please his commanding officer" (2 Timothy 2:3-4).

FRUITFUL LIVING IN THE REAL WORLD

Paul inspires me. But unlike him, I *do* have a few civilian duties that need to be taken care of every day. He wasn't married. I am. He didn't have a child. I do. What can I learn from this man that will help me live out true spirituality in the twenty-first century?

He practiced the "automatic response syndrome." Paul had a mindset that anticipated disappointments beforehand. It was no surprise to him that his demonstrative faith produced negative responses from godless people. It was the natural result of living in a fallen world.

His longing was already firmly established. His goal in life was to go and make disciples. His belief system was so firmly established in truth—God's truth—that he often "automatically" skipped a negative emotional reaction when circumstances, people, and events didn't go his way. His ruling passion was an intense love for God and his actions were a demonstration of holy zeal.

"MESS HALL" THEOLOGY

There are days when my "marching boots" are stuck in pancake syrup. My patience is thin. My love is conditional. My joy has evaporated. Peace and self-control have passed me by. On those days I need to clearly identify—by faith, not by feeling—the disappointments that produced my longing for change. Instead of "flying by my emotions," blaming the Devil or other people for my destructive actions, *I must be a responsible soldier.*

My orders are already in print. The Commander deserves my allegiance. My belief system must be checked and rechecked for misconceptions that produce ungodly ruling passions. To be completely honest is difficult. I'm tempted to go back to old patterns. I secretly like working hard for God's approval and practicing my "list mentality." But growth takes time. He knows that. I know that. And to my surprise, His abundance is mine *in* the process—not as a prize at the end of my tour of duty.

CHAPTER 12

Me—God's Woman?:
To Live Out My Reason for Being

There is no magic in small plans. When I con-
sider my ministry, I think of the world.
Anything less than that would not be worthy
of Christ nor His will for my life.
HENRIETTA MEARS

THE ABOVE statement motivates me! It's passionate. Challenging.
It's spiritually inspiring. It lets me know there are some women
who have led the way when it comes to dynamic commitment and personal sacrifice.

Henrietta Mears was a Sunday school teacher who wrote lessons for her
students. Her faithfulness in small things led to the founding of Gospel Light
Publications. Dr. Bill Bright, founder of Campus Crusade for Christ, points
to her as one of the key spiritual influences in his life. As a prayer warrior,
she was a tremendous encouragement to world-renowned evangelist Billy
Graham and many others. She was one woman with "a reason for *being.*"

Then there was Corrie ten Boom, dedicated servant of Christ. I heard
her speak to a packed auditorium on three different occasions. She said,
"I have learned in my years on earth to hold everything loosely, because

when I hold things tightly, God has to pry my fingers away. And that hurts. That hurts." Corrie had learned the secret—the essence of true spirituality. What is it? Relinquishment, plain and simple.

There was never a doubt in Corrie's mind about the work God called her to. This commission was to bear the good news of God's love, His forgiveness, and His faithfulness to the whole world. One would think that when released from Ravensbruck (a prison camp) in February, 1945, she would want to go home—to a place of safety, security, peace, and rest, surrounded by friends who would minister to her. She *deserved* that. But that thought couldn't have been further from Corrie's mind because she lived under divine constraint. She believed God commissioned her for a work.[1]

Each time I heard Corrie speak, there was a holy stirring in my soul. The message of this woman was so convicting and strong I was often moved to tears. And she didn't fit the pattern for most successful public speakers. She was overweight. Plain. Old-fashioned hair net holding gray tresses in place. Broken English. Common, homemade visual aids. No dynamic delivery techniques. So what was this woman's secret?

Corrie's secret was *a passion for God that resulted in relinquishment of her personal rights,* which included all her expectations that He should lead her along an easy path.

J. Oswald Sanders defines what we're talking about: "Spirituality is not easy to define, but its presence or absence can easily be discerned. . . . It is the power to change the atmosphere by one's presence, the unconscious influence that makes Christ and spiritual things real to others."[2]

Corrie's *disappointments* must have been overwhelming. Internment camp. The deaths of precious family members. Inhumane living conditions. Surrounded by hateful, cruel soldiers. Lice. Disease. Pain and suffering. Surely she must have *longed* for life as it was before the war. Certainly for Corrie and her family, life was not fair.

Had I been in her place, how would I have responded? My *longing* would very likely have been to escape cruelty and attempt survival by forgetting the atrocities of the war and burying myself in personal comforts and a safe haven. My *emotions* would have been evident in angry outbursts against my captors and a negative, critical attitude toward the God who allowed me to experience such brutality.

Anyone with a flawed belief system would have immediately gone through the decision-making process, arriving at an instant *ruling passion* of anger toward God. My *action* would likely have been withdrawal and isolation. Anything to forget the pain. Every lonely day would have been another opportunity for anger to breed resentment and hate in my heart toward those unfeeling people and "the God who wasn't there when I needed Him."

But not Corrie! She had *a reason for being* that went far beyond life as we know it. Her eternal mind-set was so firmly established that she looked at time here on earth as a fleeting, short prelude to eternity. I could hear her life resounding with an echo of the psalmist's words: "Hour by hour I place my days in your hand" (Psalm 31:15, MSG). Pain, suffering, even brutal existence at Ravensbruck were all a stage upon which His power could be viewed by others. God had given her a unique and special task. A high calling. He was worthy of nothing less than her all.

THE POWER OF DISAPPOINTMENT

The secret of experiencing true spirituality seems ultimately tied to how we handle our unfulfilled expectations. Do we hold our disappointments closely, fondling our hurts, ruminating over the injustices we've experienced and the unkind, unfeeling, or cruel treatment of others? That response breeds self-pity, discouragement, depression, and ultimately despair. Sometimes despair leads to suicide, and that pleases the "Father of Lies."

I believe that the greatest single cause of spiritual defeat is the Enemy's ability to get us preoccupied with our disappointments—especially personal disappointment in ourselves. We sin. We have a guilty conscience. We confess our sin. But our memory of past spiritual failure fills our visual image of "who we are." We try to work hard to please God, hoping to somehow offset the "badness" of our "real" selves—but we fail.

Now we feel guilty. We expected to feel better. But we don't. And our disappointment leads to discouragement. So we sin again . . . and again. We experience the same cycle repeatedly. We feel powerless to change.

DEALING WITH GUILT

I think David understood the pain of disappointment. I think he struggled with guilt. I'm sure he felt like a spiritual failure. After he committed adultery with Bathsheba and then saw to it that her husband, Uriah, was killed in the front lines of battle, he must have gone through an overwhelming inner struggle.

David's Expectation: He was selected above all the rest to be the king. He was "the man after God's own heart." Surely he would have expected joy, success, honor, fulfillment, and spiritual victory in his life. (I've never been a queen or even close to royalty, but I can identify with being spiritually high and feeling invincible—and expecting that feeling to last forever.)

David's Disappointment: I can only imagine the degree of David's disappointment in himself when the reality of his sin caught up with him. When confronted by the prophet Nathan, David was a broken man. Although his prayer in Psalm 51 reveals the *action* of confession following his wicked deeds, we can trace the chain reaction as he bares his soul to God:

Generous in love—God give grace! Huge in mercy—wipe out
my bad record. Scrub away my guilt, soak out my sins in your
laundry. I know how bad I've been; my sins are staring me
down. (Psalm 51:1-3, MSG)

It's pretty obvious that David was feeling heavy guilt. He had blown it. He was a marked man. Adultery. Cover-up. Murder. Scandal.

David's Emotions: Initially, his feelings must have been full of *immoral lust*. From the roof he saw a woman bathing. The woman was very beautiful, and David sent someone to find out about her. Then David sent messengers to get her. She came to him, and he slept with her (see 2 Samuel 11:2-4). Later his emotions must have swung to *fear* of being found out and then to *guilt* for having committed adultery and murdering Uriah.

David's Longing: It's hard to identify David's real longing in Scripture because he's so busy covering his tracks. Then the answer becomes obvious. His longing was for "life as it was before this major headache." His personal integrity was shot to pieces. His first son by Bathsheba died. His relationship with God was distant. Nathan the prophet was "on his case." And no matter how hard he tried to cover up his sin, it wouldn't work. (My life doesn't parallel with David's on all counts, but I do know the deep longing to "fix" my problems myself. When we long for peace in the middle of chaos, we often tend to say, "I'll do it myself, God.")

David's Belief System: In his prayer, we see David's open admission of the results that stemmed from his flawed belief system. He continues his confession with these words:

> You're the One I've violated, and you've seen it all, seen the full
> extent of my evil. . . . What you're after is truth from the inside
> out. Enter me, then; conceive a new, true life. (Psalm 51:4,6, MSG)

TRUTH IN THE INNER PARTS

And here lies the central message of this entire book. If we are ever going to experience true spirituality, we must develop a biblical belief system that will form the foundation for unshakable convictions and provide the framework for ruling passions that honor God—no matter what disappointments we experience.

I wonder what David's myths were. He might have thought:

- "I am king and I deserve it all. A little personal gratification is appropriate in my position."
- "It's easier to cover up my problems than to face them."
- "I know I'm God's chosen man, so my spiritual relationship doesn't need much maintenance."

So *how* do we develop truth in "the inner parts"? Solomon gives us the answer:

> If you accept my words and store up my commands within you, turning your ear to wisdom and applying your heart to understanding, and if you call out for insight and cry aloud for understanding, and if you look for it as for silver and search for it as for hidden treasure, then you will understand the fear of the LORD and find the knowledge of God. (Proverbs 2:1-5)

One of the functions of the Holy Spirit that I value most is His ability to give me a sense of "uneasiness" when I'm in a decision-making situation, operating with a flawed belief system. In the heat of emotion, we normally don't stop long enough to ask, "What are my firm convictions on this subject that will help to give me direction as I decide on a ruling passion and then on an action?" We're too busy reacting and throwing a royal fit because life isn't turning out the way we'd hoped it would.

So we automatically select an ungodly ruling passion and blame the resulting devastation on the rotten people in our lives, the "stupid" circumstance, or the Devil. Satan *is* powerful—very powerful—but I don't think we should blame him for *everything*.

For me, the process of "developing truth in the inner parts" begins with an acknowledgment of the Bible as the source of truth. My follow-up action must be a choice to store up His words and commands in my heart by reading and memorizing Scripture on a regular basis. (It's not easy. And it takes more discipline than I'd like to admit.) Then, when disappointments come—and they *always* do—I must stop long enough to evaluate my reaction. During that brief interlude, the Holy Spirit has an opportunity to reveal truth to me.

Because of my "humanness," that pause may come *after* my emotional outburst. It's a temptation to feel so defeated after an emotional explosion that we go back to the guilt syndrome. We think, *I've already blown it, so it doesn't really matter what my actions are.* That's a lie! We need to explore *why* the emotional reaction was so strong.

If I do wait, *before* instantly choosing a negative ruling passion, I can sift my emotions through my convictions. The pause here gives the Holy Spirit a chance to bring that sense of "uneasiness" if I'm starting to base a ruling passion on a myth. I'm beginning to appreciate that feeling. But it's hard. It's admitting I don't have all the answers. It's acknowledging that my personal spiritual journey is still very much in process. It's sacrificing ego for integrity.

The Holy Spirit becomes my teacher and guide, and responding to His leading becomes an exciting adventure. The more I take in the wisdom of God, the more accurate my belief system is and the more often my ruling passions result in honorable and holy actions.

David's Ruling Passion: Without a doubt, David made many wrong choices in his life. But after an intense struggle, David's ruling passion was his love for God.

David's Action: His action is played out in the biblical record. He chose repentance, and that resulted in a restored relationship with God and a dynamic future ministry. His prayer to His God during this time has always touched an inner chord with me:

Soak me in your laundry and I'll come out clean, scrub me and
I'll have a snow-white life. . . . God make a fresh start in me,
shape a Genesis week from the chaos of my life. (Psalm 51:7,
10-12, MSG)

There is an overwhelming joy that accompanies confession, repentance, and the restoration of close relationships with God and people we were alienated from due to our own negative ruling passions. It's humbling. Pride is put aside. Masks are removed. Honesty replaces falsehood. That which was hidden is revealed. Without confession and repentance, restoration does not occur.

But the alternative is like a cancer that attacks the body's lymph system. You never know where the next tumor will show up. You can cover the disease up for a while, but before long it always becomes visible again. The cover-up is never worth its reward. David is a perfect example of this.

RELINQUISHING OUR EXPECTATIONS
AND DISAPPOINTMENTS

For the Christian woman, life needs to be a process of relinquishing our unrealistic expectations. It's especially hard for dreamers like me. But when we dream big, disappointments fall hard. We expect too much from people and projects. And everything in us wants to hold on to our disappointments. Our personal monologue goes something like this:

- "I *believed* something would happen, and it didn't."
- "I *expected* intimacy in a friendship, and it was withheld."
- "I *knew* my marriage would be permanent, but I'm divorced."
- "I *anticipated* success in a job, and I failed."
- "I *assumed* I'd have healthy self-worth by now, but I don't."

- "I'm *convinced* God forgives sin, but I feel guilty."
- "I *thought* serving Jesus would be easy, and it's hard."

Our list could go on and on. What we expect falls short of what we experience. What we hope for in a relationship, circumstance, or event doesn't always work out. There is a gap between what we believe will take place and what actually happens. Disappointment sets in.

The essence of relinquishment is "releasing our grasp." It's giving up our rights. Surrendering our plan. Letting go. It is the hardest task of all. It goes against our natural instinct.

But our disappointments in life provide an ongoing opportunity to release our private hurts and painful memories to God.

The relinquishment of our unfulfilled expectations has the surprising potential of freeing us to experience greater intimacy with God. It's an act of trusting Him when we cannot see a positive outcome. Relinquishment puts a stop to our manipulation of other people and releases the Holy Spirit to do the supernatural through the power of prayer. Relinquishment starves little resentments that have the potential to grow into roots of bitterness.

But where do we go with our disappointments? Is there a ritual we can go through that will somehow make it easier? I'm afraid this whole idea of relinquishment requires more than I'm willing to give. I have to lay my "cherished" disappointments at the foot of Calvary and *not* pick them up again!

THE SUPREME EXAMPLE

What was it like for the Son of God to experience the ultimate disappointment? The only man in history to be born without sin was asked by His Father to pay the penalty for all of mankind. He had experience with handling the disappointments of others. When people followed Him because they expected to get free bread, He exposed their wrong motives. When they expected to crown Him king, He quietly disappeared from among them.

Then it happened. He had that final meal with the Twelve. All that talk about the coming of the Comforter, about the vine and branches, and about how they should love each other, they didn't understand. He was so serious. He talked about leaving, but He spoke with expectant hope about coming back. Why, if He was coming back, did He give this long speech at the dinner table that night?

It was time to go. He took his intimate friends—Peter, James, and John. He would need them to pray there at the Mount of Olives. Surely He could count on them. Out of His sad awareness of what the next day held, Jesus bared His heart to His best friends. "This sorrow is crushing my life out. Stay here and keep vigil with me" (Matthew 26:38, MSG). But when He returned, they were sleeping. It happened three times in a row.

Withdrawing from them, He fell to the ground and prayed, "My Father, if there is any way, get me out of this" (Matthew 26:39, MSG).

I can almost hear Him pleading, "Father, is there *any* other way than the cross?" *At that moment in time, did Jesus have an expectation that just maybe He wouldn't have to face the crucifixion?*

Then, almost instantaneously, He relinquished His own rights, and we hear Him say, "But please, not what I want. You, what do *you* want?" (Matthew 26:39, MSG).

For Jesus, the decision was immediate. He knew His mission—a special task for which He alone was chosen. His longing was to please the Father. His convictions were set in truth. Surrendering His rights, He relinquished any hold on the thought that there might be another alternative that would make it possible for you and me to experience forgiveness of sin and intimacy with God. There was no other way. With a ruling passion of love, His action of obedience unto death—even death on a cross cemented for all time His *reason for being*.

LIVING OUT MY REASON FOR BEING

I'm not Corrie ten Boom. I'm just a regular kind of woman trying to be a "for-real" Christian in twenty-first-century America. I remember wondering if God talked to Corrie out loud. She seemed to hear Him so clearly. I long for that.

If we could talk face-to-face, I wonder what He'd say to me. Right now, in the middle of my ordinary days, am I accomplishing His purpose for my life? Am I living out His reason for creating me? Do I have *a passion for God?*

I wonder if I'm getting any closer to *true spirituality* than I was last year. With all my heart, I don't want to be an ordinary Christian. He deserves more. I chuckle at that lofty thought. My fingers are in peanut butter and my phone is ringing and someone is at the door. But then I remember. God has always used ordinary people to carry out His extraordinary mission.

J. Oswald Sanders was right. True spirituality is the power to change the atmosphere by our presence. It's *the unconscious influence* that makes Christ and spiritual things real to others. That must mean that *being fully woman and fully God's* can, over time, become as natural as breathing.

True spirituality means relinquishing our expectations and disappointments to Him. It's being "like a tree planted by the water"—and sinking deep roots. The psalmist reminds us that God "satisfies the thirsty and fills the hungry with good things" (Psalm 107:9).

Lord, be glorified in me. Let Your supernatural presence be felt by the people in my life. Free me from false guilt. Establish my heart in truth. Help me to encourage others on their journey home. Give me the boldness to speak and the wisdom to be quiet. Let Your creativity flow through me. But center my lofty thoughts on You. Teach me the value of solitude. Slow me down. Quiet my heart. Give me an eternal mind-set. Purify my motives. Keep me from demanding visible results. Teach me to pray. Guard my convictions. Let my ruling passion be my love for You. Amen.

Twelve-Week Bible Study for Secret Longings of the Heart

WEEK 1

Read chapter 1, "Hidden Longings of the Heart."

1. If you are meeting with a group, give your name and then describe one thing about you that would surprise most people. (Examples: You *love* chocolate. You were born in a foreign country. You are shy. You have been on a diet for your entire adult life.)

2. Memorize Psalm 38:9 (NIV). Write it out on a 3 x 5 card and carry it with you this week. Rehearse the verse while you wait at red lights. Try taping the verse to the side of your computer or above your kitchen sink. If you are meeting with a group, read the verse aloud together: "All my longings lie open before you, O Lord; my sighing is not hidden from you."

   a. Have you ever had a friend with whom you could share your deepest longings and painful disappointments? If so, describe some of the characteristics of that friend.

   b. What does it mean to you that God knows *all* your longings and that He even hears your *sighing*? Is that thought comforting or frightening to you?

3. In the form of a prayer, write a list of your longings to God. For instance, "Lord, my heart desires a closer relationship with You. I also long for better communication with my child/friend/spouse. I sincerely want to find a job that makes my heart sing," and so on. If you're meeting with a group, have a few volunteers read their prayers aloud.

4. Read the definition of passion on page 13.

   a. When you hear or read the word *passion,* what comes to your mind?

   b. Is the word *passion* a positive word or a negative word to you? Why?

   c. Read the story of Carol's friend Deb on pages 11-12. Deb asked, "What makes you weep and pound the table?" How do you answer that question?

   d. Describe a person you know or someone you have met who exemplifies what it means to be a passionate Christian woman.

5. All of us experience emotional stress and spiritual conflict because of two basic facts:

- Women (and men) are created in the image of God. Read Genesis 1:27. (See page 13.)
- Sin entered the human race in the Garden of Eden. (See page 13.)

When we sin, we feel alienated from God. How would you rate your intimacy with God right now, with 1 being the furthest away and 10 representing a close relationship with regular time spent in the Word of God and in honest, vulnerable prayer?

   1   2   3   4   5   6   7   8   9   10

far from God   close to God

6. Read the basic facts about God on page 14 that help us understand how we can experience closeness with Him. Do you remember a time in your life when you made a personal faith commitment to Jesus Christ? If so, when was that? If you're meeting with a group, have a couple of volunteers share their experiences.

7. Read Psalm 42:1-2: "As the deer pants for streams of water, so my soul pants for you, O God. My soul thirsts for God, for the living God. When can I go and meet with God?"

a. Do you remember a time in your life when you longed for a more personal intimacy with God? Describe your experience.

b. Do you have a favorite place where you like to meet with God? (For example, do you have a room in your house or a spot outside that has become a favorite location for spending time with Him?)

8. Answer the following questions on your own. If you're meeting with a group, read the questions aloud and ask group members to answer them on their own during the week.

a. What are the aches in my heart that have never been touched?

b. Do I have hidden, negative emotions that have been covered over with denial or feverish work?

c. Is there anyone I dislike, hate, envy, resent, or fear?

d. Am I living for a purpose that transcends my daily routine and problems?

e. How do I usually handle my disappointments?

9. Read Psalm 37:4: "Delight yourself in the LORD and he will give you the desires of your heart."

a. What do you think that verse means?

b. What one thing will you do this week that demonstrates "delighting in the Lord?"

WEEK 2

Read chapter 2, "Secret Passions—Destructive, Honorable, or Holy?"

1. When you were a child, what were your expectations about what you wanted to "be" as an adult?

2. Memorize Jeremiah 29:11-13: "'For I know the plans I have for you,' declares the LORD, 'plans to prosper you and not to harm you, plans to give you hope and a future. Then you will call upon me and come and pray to me, and I will listen to you. You will seek me and find me when you seek me with all your heart.'" Speak the verse aloud as a group. Make a habit of writing each week's verse on a Post-It note or 3 x 5 card and putting it in a visible place. In the car this week, say it out loud when you are waiting at stoplights.

a. What are God's plans for you, according to this Scripture passage?

b. According to these verses, how can we find God?

3. There are five key types of longings that produce tremendous passion within us. Read through the descriptions on pages 28-31.

a. Of these five longings of the Christian woman, which one best represents a desire you have in your life right now?

b. How can our longings get us into trouble?

There's a chain reaction all of us go through when we face disappointments and unfulfilled expectations. Here's what we experience:

Expectation
(can be innate or learned)

Disappointment
(what we experience when what we hope for falls short of what we got)

Longing
(we think we're longing for what we expected in the first place)

Emotions
(we respond emotionally based on our individual personalities)

Belief System
(we run our emotions through this grid)

Ruling Passion
(a decision is made based on our spiritual condition)

Action
(the final step that will result in activity that is holy, honorable, or destructive)

As you study this chain reaction, what part of the process has the potential for getting you into the most trouble?

4. When you respond emotionally to your disappointments, which of the following best describes you?

- **The Hot Reactor** (If Mama ain't happy, ain't nobody happy! All emotions are out on the table. No one has to guess where you stand because you tell them, but you get over negative reactions quickly.)
- **The Slow Boiler** (You pack little disappointments away emotionally and finally blow up after "just one more thing" puts you over the edge.)
- **The Stuffer** (Due to the pain, hurt, or abuse of the past, you stuff and deny negative emotions because giving yourself permission to "feel" hurts too much.)

5. Read pages 25-26 and write a brief description of the following words:

a. Destructive Passions

b. Honorable Passions

c. Holy Passions

6. When we dream big, disappointments fall hard. Read the following list of disappointments. Which ones have you experienced?

- "I *believed* something would happen, and it didn't."
- "I *expected* intimacy in a friendship, and it was withheld."
- "I *knew* my marriage would be permanent, but I'm divorced."
- "I *anticipated* success in a job, and I failed."
- "I *assumed* I'd have healthy self-worth by now, but I don't."
- "I'm *convinced* God forgives sin, but I feel guilty."
- "I *thought* serving Jesus would be easy, and it's hard."

7. Write down one of your deepest disappointments. (This could involve relationships, career situations, ministry opportunities, personal discipline failures, or hoped-for events or opportunities that didn't materialize.)

a. How did you react emotionally?

b. Did this disappointment lead you to take action? If so, what did you do?

c. What spiritual lessons did you learn during the waiting times?

8. Read the following verses and summarize them below:

James 1:5

Ecclesiastes 7:25

9. Write down one way you will seek wisdom this week as you embark on understanding the deepest longings of your heart.

WEEK 3

Read chapter 3, "I Want to Feel Special."

1. Who made you feel significant as a child or young adult? How did this person give you a sense of value and respect?

2. Memorize Genesis 1:27: "So God created man in his own image, in the image of God he created him; male and female he created them." Keep a copy of this verse with you throughout the week and speak the words aloud until the Scripture is memorized.

   a. Summarize the core message of this verse.

   b. How does the truth of this verse affect your sense of worth?

3. Did you have any nicknames as a child? If so, how were you positively and/or negatively affected by what you were called?

4. Feeling significant is a lifelong battle for most of us. We have an urgent need to know beyond any doubt that we are personally important to God and that He has something important for us to do with our time, talent, and energy.

   On the following scale, circle the number that best represents how significant you felt as a child. If you are doing this study with a group, share the number you circled.

   1   2   3   4   5   6   7   8   9   10
   I felt like a nobody.   I felt valued and loved.

   Why did you choose that number?

5. Read the following Scripture references and write down key words, phrases, and concepts that validate your own significance to God.

   Psalm 16:11

   Psalm 139:13-16

   Romans 12:4-8

   Philippians 1:6

6. In 1861 Emily Dickinson wrote,

> I'm Nobody! Who are you?
> Are you—Nobody too?
> Then there's a pair of us! Don't tell!
> They'd advertise—you know.[1]

Does it surprise you that women have been struggling over their sense of significance for over two hundred years? Why or why not?

7. Read the following Scripture references and make notes on these Bible characters. How was their feeling of significance affected by their circumstances and how they viewed their own giftedness?

a. Moses after being asked to lead the nation of Israel

Exodus 4:10

b. Joshua after being told that he would be following Moses as leader of the nation of Israel

Deuteronomy 34:10,12; Joshua 1:1-2

c. David overwhelmed with opportunities God opened in his life

2 Samuel 7:18-19

d. Elijah after God destroyed 450 prophets of Baal, but Jezebel had threatened his life

1 Kings 19:3-4

e. Jeremiah—at the time of being told by God he was chosen to be a prophet

Jeremiah 1:6

8. Sue Monk Kidd said, "The deepest need of the human heart is to be loved. To be loved utterly and completely just as we are, no matter what."[2] Do you agree or disagree with this statement? Why?

9. Read the description on pages 46-47 of the five crucial elements in significance that authors Gary Smalley and John Trent identify in *The Blessing.* Which of the five elements has been the most important in your life when it comes to feeling significant to God?

10. Read 1 Peter 2:9: "But you are a chosen people, a royal priest-hood, a holy nation, a people belonging to God, that you may declare the praises of him who called you out of darkness into his wonderful light."

a. Summarize the ways in which God values people who belong to Him.

b. Think of one woman you know who needs to be reminded of her value to God and to you. This week, find a way to let her know how significant she is. (You could do this through a card, a call, or an e-mail note.)

WEEK 4

Read chapter 4, "I Want to Do Something Worthwhile."

1. When someone you've met asks, "And what do you do for a living?" how do you normally respond? How do you feel about the question?

2. Memorize Jeremiah 31:3: "'I have loved you with an everlasting love; I have drawn you with loving-kindness.'" Write the verse out on a Post-It note and put it in a place where you will see it often. Speak the words out loud slowly. Close your eyes and see if you can remember portions of the verse already.

a. Based on this verse, how long will God love you?

b. How has God demonstrated His loving-kindness to you in the past?

3. Read the first story in chapter 4, on pages 49-50.

a. Has there ever been a time in your life when you equated what you do for a living with who you are as a person? Explain.

b. Looking back on your life, what events, comments, or situations robbed you of your sense of worth? How did you react as a result of feeling low self-esteem?

4. Think about the work you do in an average day (whether or not you get paid for it). Experts define work as "purposeful activity" that is revealed in *expression*—that which expresses our abilities; *provision*—that which provides for our needs; and *mission*—that which accomplishes God's agenda on this earth. On the scale below, evaluate how significant you feel with your work. To what degree do you feel you are using your best gifts for honorable and holy purposes?

1	2	3	4	5	6	7	8	9	10
low significance									high significance

If you're meeting with a group, share the number you chose and why you chose it.

5. Elijah felt worthless, even though with God's help he destroyed hundreds of prophets of Baal. (You can read the whole story in 1 Kings 18–19:4.) One woman (Jezebel) threatened his life and he ran a day's journey into the desert and prayed that he would die.

a. Have you ever wanted to "throw in the towel" because of unusual stress in work, ministry, or life? If so, describe that time.

b. Read 1 Kings 19:5-9. What did Elijah need?

c. The next few verses reveal that the word of the Lord did not come in the wind, the earthquake, or the fire; it came in a gentle whisper (1 Kings 19:11-12). Have you ever believed God spoke to your heart in an unexpected way and gave you strength for what you faced next? Explain.

6. Read Jeremiah 1:1-9.

a. What did God ask Jeremiah to do?

b. What was Jeremiah's response?

c. What words did the Lord use to build up Jeremiah's confidence?

7. Read the following statements. Which one is most meaningful to you as you seek to follow God's leading for your future? Explain.

- God has a plan for my life that will maximize the use of my gifts for His kingdom.
- God reveals His call on my life after I confess all sin in my heart, verbalize my openness to His plan for my life, and make my life available for His direction.
- God's call on my life will be confirmed through His Word and through His Spirit.
- God often affirms His call through the affirmation of people who are close to Him.
- God's call always involves a cost—being willing to die to my own plans and selfish desires.[3]

8. Read Psalm 32:8.

a. What hope does this verse give you for the decisions you need to make about your future?

b. What woman will you encourage this week (via a call, e-mail note, or personal visit) to let her know you are praying for her about choices she needs to make?

WEEK 5

Read chapter 5, "Why Me? Why This? Why Now?"

1. What question would you like to ask God about why He allowed something to happen that didn't make any sense to you?

2. Memorize 1 Peter 4:12-13: "Dear friends, do not be surprised at the painful trial you are suffering, as though something strange were happening to you. But rejoice that you participate in the sufferings of Christ, so that you may be overjoyed when His glory is revealed." Write the verse out and rehearse it out loud this week when you are in the car or alone in your home.

a. Summarize the main points of the verse.

Suffering is normal — Christ also suffered

b. Why do you think we shouldn't be surprised that bad things sometimes happen to good Christian people?

it is an imperfect world —

3. Think back to the last time you experienced a crisis that deeply rocked your sense of security. Did an older Christian put an arm around you and say, "We know that all things work together for good to them that love God" (Romans 8:28, KJV)? If something similar has happened to you, evaluate your emotional reaction to the person's comments.

1	2	3	4	5	6	7	8	9	10
angry and resentful					totally accepting and grateful toward this individual for the wise counsel				

a. What do you think Romans 8:28 means?

b. Does Romans 8:29 shed any light on the meaning of the verse that preceded it? Explain.

4. Read the story of Carol's miscarriage on pages 66-69.

a. The flawed values system she was using was based on a number of myths she had come to believe. Put a check in each box that represents a "myth" you have struggled with in your own life.

☐ If I'm a good Christian, life should be fair.
☐ It's a sin to feel depressed.
☐ If I am living in fellowship with God, I should never feel anger toward Him or other people.
☐ If God loved me, bad things would not happen to me.
☐ When there is so much real tragedy in the world, it's wrong for me to feel grief over little things.

b. Comment on one of the myths you've struggled with.

5. Have you ever had an experience in which you felt disappointed with God?

6. Read Job 30:20,26-27. Have you ever been as honest as Job was with God about your disappointment regarding undesired changes

in your life that resulted in emotional or physical pain? Is it hard
for you to talk to Him in this way? Why or why not?

yes – hard to talk anyone todly

7. Read the following Scripture verses and summarize the truth you
find.

Philippians 1:29

James 1:2

Psalm 34:18

8. Renewing your mind with the Word of God is an important part
of building a biblical belief system. Read Proverbs 2:1-5.

a. According to this verse, how can a person find the knowledge
of God?

b. What piece of knowledge have you learned doing this lesson
that you will share with someone else this week?

WEEK SIX

Read chapter 6, "Lord, Make Me Flexible!"

1. Someone once defined change as "anything that rocks my boat." What is one change that has rocked your boat at some time in your life? (Examples: moving to another location, a new job, having a baby, a health crisis for you or a family member, a child in rebellion)

2. Memorize 2 Corinthians 4:16-17: "Therefore we do not lose heart. Though outwardly we are wasting away, yet inwardly we are being renewed day by day. For our light and momentary troubles are achieving for us an eternal glory that far outweighs them all." Write out the verse and, as you review it this week, share it with a friend or family member in person, by phone, or in an e-mail note.

Juding by eternity

3. Read the definitions of the following phrases on page 81 and next to the words, write a description of that type of change.

   a. Anticipated Changes

   b. Unexpected Changes

c. No Changes

Incomplete parts

Which category is the most difficult for you? Why do you suppose that's the case?

4. Place a check next to each of the following changes you have experienced within the last year.

☐ Change in housing

☑ Change in employment (new job, loss of job, change in job description)

☐ Change in family situation (new marriage, new baby, relatives moving in or out)

☐ Change in churches

☑ Change in your health or that of a close family member

☐ Change in finances

☑ Change in a relationship with a person you value

☐ Change in "life situation" due to something unexpected

Which change brought you the greatest loss of security? Why?

5. Read Philippians 4:11-13.

a. What had the apostle Paul learned about dealing with points of change in his life?

b. What did he know about God that enabled him to get his security from God?

6. Paul experienced beatings, imprisonment, shipwreck, and persecution. Read 2 Corinthians 4:8-9,18. Do you think Paul ever doubted God's love when he went through the "tough times" in his life? Explain.

7. Read pages 90-91. Which of the following statements is the most difficult one for you to embrace? Why?

• I cannot always be in control of every situation in my life.
• Just because God does not alleviate my current pain does not mean He does not love me.
• Admitting my doubts about God to someone else is not a sin.

8. Exodus describes a battle between the Israelites and the Amalekites. When Moses held up his hands, the Israelites were winning, but whenever he lowered his hands, the other side started winning. Read Exodus 17:12.

a. What did Aaron and Hur do for Moses and what was the result?

b. How easy is it for you to lean on others? Why is that?

9. Identify someone you know who is going through a deep disappointment or crisis of faith.

   a. Pray for her need.

   b. How can you come alongside as a support person? What will you do this week to assist this individual?

WEEK SEVEN

Read chapter 7, "Please Hear Me!"

1. Experts in communication say we need about twelve touches a day to feel loved and valued. Did you grow up in a home where there was appropriate touching, or were you raised in a family that showed very little outward affection? How did your upbringing affect your ability to relate to other people when you became an adult?

2. Memorize John 15:12-13: "'My command is this: Love each other as I have loved you. Greater love has no one than this, that he lay down his life for his friends.'" Write out the verse on a Post-It note. Repeat the verse slowly and think about one person in your life who is easy to love and one person who is hard to love. Pray for both of these people every time you review your memory verse this week.

3. Read the first story in chapter 7, on pages 97-100.

a. Have you ever been disappointed in the response of someone you tried to befriend? How did you respond?

b. What do you think is the difference between loneliness and solitude?

4. Read through the fifteen elements of a close friendship. Check the boxes next to five items on the list that are the most important to you in a friendship. Share one of them with the group, and tell why it is important to you.

☐ A deep care and concern for me personally

☑ A personality I enjoy (intelligence, spiritual depth, and a great sense of humor)

☐ An active interest in and support of my projects and dreams

☐ An instinct to automatically come alongside and help when I am in need

☑ A spiritual bonding as friends (hard to define, but your heart tells you when it's there)

☐ An "instant availability" when true emergencies demand momentary inconvenience

☑ A commitment to each other, while allowing the other person to enjoy the freedom of time alone, other friendships, and individual personhood

☑ A compassionate heart that cheers when I succeed and feels my pain when I fail

☐ A tangible support through communication (often enough so I feel valued, but infrequently enough so I don't feel strangled)

☑ An ability to lovingly confront me with hard questions that hold
me accountable for spiritual growth and personal integrity

☐ A listening ear—someone attentive who will really hear me

☐ A heart for God's Word and an eager interest in ministry-related
activities

☐ A powerful prayer partner

☐ An affirming encourager

☐ An individual who can expect all of this from me without making me feel the "weight" of obligation if I don't measure up

5. Read 1 Samuel 18:1,3-4 and pages 105-107 about the covenant
relationship David and Jonathan had with each other.

a. Describe their relationship.

b. How do we demonstrate our friendship to people we care
about in today's world?

6. Read the descriptions of the stealers of intimacy on pages 109-110.

a. Write down the "intimacy stealer" that has caused you the greatest challenge.

b. What is one thing you'd like to work on with God's help so
that you'll be better able to draw close to people?

7. Read Ephesians 4:29.

   a. How can we "build others up according to their needs"?

   b. What does the term *unwholesome talk* mean? What does it do
   to the intimacy in a friendship?

8. Read Proverbs 27:6. Have you ever had a friend honestly confront
   you about something you needed to deal with in your life? If so,
   how did you react, and what did this incident do to your friendship?

9. Read Proverbs 27:17.

   a. Who is a model to you of someone who sharpens her spiritual
   and intellectual skills with others?

   b. Make an "iron sharpening iron" appointment with a friend this
   week (even if it's by phone). Have a written agenda that will
   lead you to talk about how Christian women can "sharpen"
   each other.

WEEK 8

Read chapter 8, "Please Hold Me!"

1. What does the word *cherish* mean to you? How important do you think it is to most women to feel cherished by someone?

2. Memorize Psalm 103:17: "From everlasting to everlasting the LORD's love is with those who fear him, and his righteousness with their children's children—with those who keep his covenant and remember to obey his precepts." Write out the verse and repeat it throughout the week until you can recite it from memory.

   a. Why is it important to know that the Lord's love is "from everlasting to everlasting"?

   b. What do we need to do to experience that love?

   c. Do you think this verse demands that we obey perfectly all the time? What makes you say that?

3. On the following scale, indicate how intimate you think your relationship with God is right now.

1	2	3	4	5	6	7	8	9	10
I feel far from God.				It's been better.			I feel close to God.		

How have you tried to develop intimacy with God?

4. Your memory verse for week four was Jeremiah 31:3: "I have loved you with an everlasting love; I have drawn you with loving-kindness." List all of the ways in which you feel *cherished* by God. Then thank Him for each item on your list.

5. Read the first story in chapter 8 about Nancy's expectation, disappointment, and ruling passion that led to an adulterous relationship. Where do you think her problem started? What fueled her destructive choice?

6. Whether you are married or single, place a check in the box next to every disappointment you can identify with. (You will not be asked to share your answers with the group.)

☐ I don't feel cherished.

☐ My husband never really talks to me.

☐ There's no romance in my life.

☐ I always thought I'd be married, but I'm not.

☐ My husband and I never get away from all our pressures long enough to have fun together.

☐ I don't remember the last time my husband just held me close and listened to my needs.

☐ My husband doesn't seem to care if I enjoy our physical relationship or not; he just wants to satisfy himself.

☐ My husband has forgotten how to dream with me about the future.

Do you agree or disagree with the following statement? "When enough of our disappointments betray our expectations, we are open to temptation in the area of sexual immorality."

7. Read the following verses and summarize the main thought in each passage.

Genesis 2:24-25

1 Corinthians 7:3-5

Hebrews 13:4

8. Turn to pages 124-126 and read the descriptions of the five reasons women often give when they choose a ruling passion of immorality.

a. Which of these five areas do you think is the biggest problem for women today?

b. What are some specific ways friends can hold each other accountable for purity in their behavior, attitudes, and thoughts?

9. Read Ecclesiastes 4:9-10. Call or get together with a friend this week and discuss the following building blocks that help us "hold tight" to those we love:

- Time
- My personal relationship with God
- Conflict and resolution
- Tenderness given and received
- Trust given and received

Speak honestly with each other about how important each item is to you, whether you are struggling in this area, Scripture verses that would be of help, and a growth step you could take.

WEEK NINE

Read chapter 9, "I Blew It Again!"

1. Which of the following words or phrases best describes how you would like other people to perceive you: organized, disciplined, intelligent, good parent, high achiever, spiritual, kind, honest, vulnerable? Why did you choose the words you did?

2. Memorize Ephesians 2:10: "For we are God's workmanship, created in Christ Jesus to do good works, which God prepared in advance for us to do." Write the verse on a Post-It note and place it near the telephone you most often use. This week, every time you prepare to make a call, read the verse first.

a. Describe what it means to you to be "God's workmanship." What qualifies someone for that title?

b. Name some works you believe God "prepared in advance" for you to do.

3. Read the first story in chapter 9, on pages 135-137.

a. What do you typically do when you're under pressure?

☐ Scream
☐ Give people the silent treatment
☐ Pretend you're fine
☐ Cry
☐ Apologize for your failings
☐ Lightheartedly admit your limitations
☐ Other:

b. Tell about a time when you tried to appear organized, "together," or impressive when things weren't going your way. What action did you take?

4. Read the description of "The Seven Woes to the Pharisees" from Matthew 23 on page 142.

a. What similarities do you see in yourself?

b. How do you think God's expectations about your performance differ from the perfectionistic lists of the Pharisees?

5. Read Romans 8:26-27 and summarize the truths that are stated in those verses.

6. Read the following statements silently and mark them true or false. Then, if you're meeting with a group, you may take turns reading the statements aloud and then let members of the group share their thoughts regarding each item. Be ready to discuss your responses to these statements.

True False

☐ ☐ My disappointments often lead me to a negative attitude.

☐ ☐ I sometimes hold back from trying something new because of a fear of failure.

☐ ☐ I am in a ministry and/or career that could keep me challenged and happy for the rest of my life.

☐ ☐ I would like to get more formal education.

☐ ☐ Most of my Christian friends don't scream at their children.

☐ ☐ I should be content to continue working in a job beneath my potential because it develops true Christian humility.

☐ ☐ A lot of Christian women who do not work outside the home misunderstand the motives of Christian women who do work outside the home.

7. The female "success model" we frequently refer to is the woman of Proverbs 31. The reason we are sometimes overwhelmed by (and perhaps a bit irritated with) this woman is that she *appears* to be "perfect," which is far different from what we know ourselves to be.

a. Read Proverbs 31:10-31 and write down anything you discover about this woman in relation to the following:

Her husband

Her children

Her giftedness

Her energy level

Her demonstration of charity

Her tongue

Her response to old age

Her faith in God

b. What do you see as the most important aspect of this woman's success? Why?

c. Does this woman seem more "liberated" or more "restricted" than you feel right now? Explain.

8. One of the best ways to transcend failure is to do an act of kindness for someone else. Write down a specific action you will take

this week to ease someone's burden. (Ideas: baby-sit for a single parent, visit a prisoner, read to an elderly person)

WEEK TEN

Read chapter 10, "Self-Actualization?"

1. What is the most meaningful compliment you can remember receiving? Did it make you feel successful?

2. Memorize Psalm 16:11 (KJV): "Thou wilt shew me the path of life: in thy presence is fullness of joy; at thy right hand there are pleasures for evermore." Write the verse out and put it on the visor of your car. Rehearse it aloud every time you get in the car, wait at a red light, or get stuck in traffic this week.

   a. What does this verse promise?

   b. Name some of the pleasures you have experienced as a Christian woman.

3. Read the summaries on page 148 of "the changing times" for women living through the decades described there. If you could

change time, in which of the decades (if any) would you prefer to live your life? Why?

4. Even though the choices and responsibilities may be more challenging than ever before, what are the advantages and disadvantages the Christian woman has in the new millennium?

5. Read the following list of disappointments. Place a check in the box next to each one with which you identify. If you are studying with a group, share which disappointments and/or feelings you most identify with.

☐ Desiring to try different employment, but held back by economic limitations and fear of failure

☐ Hoping to do something extraordinary with my time and talents, but feeling "average.

☐ Longing for parents and/or friends to accept my personal choice to be "self-actualized" at home, but disappointed by their negative response

☐ Wanting Christians to understand the compatibility of a business career with the role of a Christian wife or pastor's wife, but feeling judged and rejected

☐ Wishing for educational opportunities and the resulting self-esteem, but held back by the constraints of time, responsibilities, and fear

☐ Expecting to be in a fulfilling job, but feeling unchallenged and a bit unspiritual for being restless

6. Read Psalm 5:1-3. On the scale below, indicate how you feel about being honest with God about your disappointments regarding your passion for success and fulfillment. Share your response with the group.

1	2	3	4	5	6	7	8	9	10
embarrassed and uneasy							comfortable and understood		

7. Flawed beliefs produce low self-worth. Read the following statements and place a check in the box next to each "myth" you struggle with presently or have struggled with in the past.

   ☐ I am only as good as my job description.

   ☐ Because I'm a Christian, God will always make me happy in my work.

   ☐ If other people don't approve of my choices, I must be wrong.

   ☐ God will love me more if I'm "above average."

   ☐ If I got poor grades as a kid, I'm unintelligent.

   ☐ If I try something new and fail, I'm out of God's will.

   ☐ Feeling creative restlessness in my work means I'm discontented with God.

   Which of the untrue statements has been the most difficult for you to delete from your belief system? Why?

8. Read and paraphrase Psalm 51:6.

9. Sometime this week, write out your answers to the following questions. Get together with a friend or a member of your Bible

study and discuss your answers. Or e-mail your responses to each other.

a. What causes most of my frustration, anxiety, and pressure?

b. What produces most of my fun, pleasure, and enjoyment?

c. Why am I doing the job I'm doing? (If it's only for the money, that's not good enough.)

d. If I could do anything I wanted, without the restrictions of time, money, education, or current responsibilities, what would it be?

e. What are my greatest strengths?

f. What would I like to do for God in my lifetime?

WEEK ELEVEN

Read chapter 11, "Whatever the Abundant Life Is, I Want It!"

1. As a young adult, what was (or is) your description of an "ideal" life? How does it differ from your "real" life? --

2. Memorize John 10:10: "I have come that they may have life, and have it to the full." Write the verse out and rehearse it out loud until you are able to remember the Scripture and the reference without looking it up. Describe on paper what "life to the full" means to you at this stage of your life.

3. Read the first story in chapter 11 (about Julie), on pages 165-167. Married or single, we all have circumstances, events, and people who shoot holes in our spiritual balloon.

   a. In what ways do you personally identify with Julie in that illustration?

   b. When have you longed for spiritual growth in your family or yourself, but instead of improving, things got worse or just didn't change? How did you deal with that disappointment?

c. Have you ever had the experience of "blowing up" with such emotional force that you surprised even yourself? If so, how did you feel afterward?

4. Take turns reading through the following list of misconceptions that sometimes get subtly ingrained in our values. Place a mark in the box next to each item you have struggled with in the past.

☐ God can't use me unless I'm a spiritual giant.

☐ If I work hard, God will give me success in my ministry.

☐ It's my Christian duty to be perfect.

☐ Visible results are the measuring stick of spiritual effectiveness.

☐ I could do more for God if my family were more spiritual and if I were more talented.

☐ The abundant Christian life is always filled with adrenaline-producing highs.

☐ I would be a better Christian if my husband loved Jesus more. (You may substitute mother, father, sister, brother, or friend for the word *husband*.)

Which of these misconceptions has been the most difficult for you to overcome, and why?

5. Developing a passion for God means facing reality by comparing our misconceptions with what the Bible actually says. Read Jeremiah 17:7-8. According to this verse, how can a person be blessed? What does this look like in practice?

Oak of rightaeoness —

6. Read through the following list and circle the item that represents your most difficult personal challenge. If you're meeting with a group, share your thoughts.

- Fear
- Anxiety
- Workaholism
- Perfectionism
- Negative attitudes
- Manipulation of others (This is very subtle, so you may not realize you are doing it. Ask a trusted friend to tell you the truth.)

7. When you think about being "like a tree planted by the water that sends out its roots by the stream," what comes to your mind? Discuss one of the ways you will continue to develop a "spiritual root system" this week.

8. Read 2 Timothy 2:3-4. What is one thing you can do this week to please your "commanding officer"?

WEEK TWELVE

Read chapter 12, "Me—God's Woman?"

1. Write brief responses to the following questions:

   a. What speaker or writer has God used to impact your life in a powerful way?

b. What book (other than the Bible) has been a tremendous help in your Christian growth?

c. What two words would you like other people to associate with you? (You do not have to be living up to the ideal represented by the words in order to write them down. However, as other people view your life, how would you like to be identified?)

If you're meeting with a group, pair off and take a few minutes to share your responses to these questions.

2. Memorize 2 Corinthians 10:5 (MSG): "We use our powerful God-tools for smashing warped philosophies, tearing down barriers erected against the truth of God, fitting every loose thought and emotion and impulse into the structure of life shaped by Christ." Write the verse.

a. What is your method for recognizing "warped philosophies"?

b. How can you fit "every loose thought and emotion and impulse into the structure of life shaped by Christ"?

3. J. Oswald Sanders said, "Spirituality is not easy to define, but its presence or absence can easily be discerned. . . . It is the power to change the atmosphere by one's presence, the unconscious influence that makes Christ and spiritual things real to others."[4]

   a. What contemporary woman do you think best demonstrates J. Oswald Sanders' description of spirituality? Describe her characteristics.

   b. How has this woman deepened your desire to have a passion for God?

   c. What female Bible character is an example for you of a woman with a zeal for God? Explain why you see her this way.

4. Do you ever feel there is a great difference between the "spiritual person" you desire to be and the reality of who you are? Explain.

5. Read Matthew 28:19-20. Most of us know we should witness to nonChristians. On a scale of 1 to 10, how do you rate your current effectiveness in personal evangelism?

   1   2   3   4   5   6   7   8   9   10
   I never witness.   I occasionally witness.   I frequently witness.

6. The Bible is our source of truth. Look back at each of the five major longings in this study and list one of your memory verses or an idea that emphasizes an important truth you learned.

a. The Longing for Significance

b. The Longing for Security

c. The Longing for Intimacy

d. The Longing for Success

e. The Longing for Spirituality

7. What has God been speaking to your heart about during the twelve weeks of this study?

8. As women with a passion for God, we have the great privilege of influencing younger women. Make a list of three women in your

current sphere of influence. List some specific things you can do to make Christ and spiritual things real to them. (Examples: baby-sit for a mother with preschoolers, start a Bible study in your neighborhood, invite someone to lunch who is not already one of your close friends, have a "welcome tea" for your new neighbor)

9. If you're meeting with a group, spend some time in prayer together. End your prayer time by reading the following prayer together:

"Lord, be glorified in me. Let Your supernatural presence be felt by the people in my life. Free me from false guilt. Establish my heart in truth. Help me to encourage others on their journey home. Give me the boldness to speak and the wisdom to be quiet. Let your creativity flow through me. But center my lofty thoughts on You. Teach me the value of solitude. Slow me down. Quiet my heart. Give me an eternal mindset. Purify my motives. Keep me from demanding visible results. Teach me to pray. Guard my convictions. Let my ruling passion be my love for you. Amen."

Notes

❧ ❧

CHAPTER 1: HIDDEN LONGINGS OF THE HEART
1. *Webster's New World Dictionary of the American Language,*
   s.v. "passion."

CHAPTER 2: SECRET PASSIONS—DESTRUCTIVE, HONORABLE, OR HOLY?
1. Quoted from a cassette tape by Miss A. Wetherell Johnson, from one
   of her Bible Study Fellowship lessons.

CHAPTER 3: I WANT TO FEEL SPECIAL
1. Opening quotation from Emily Dickinson, *The Complete Poems of
   Emily Dickinson,* Thomas H. Johnson ed., copyrighted in 1960 by
   Mary L. Hampson (Boston: Little, Brown and Company, 1960), p. 133.
2. Francis Schaeffer, source unknown.
3. James Dobson, *What Wives Wish Their Husbands Knew About
   Women* (Wheaton, Ill.: Tyndale House, 1975), pp. 22-23.
4. Gary Smalley and John Trent, *The Blessing* (Nashville: Thomas
   Nelson, 1986), p. 24.
5. Sue Monk Kidd, *God's Joyful Surprise* (New York: Harper & Row,
   1987), p. 3.
6. Kidd, p. 125.

CHAPTER 4: I WANT TO DO SOMETHING WORTHWHILE
1. Bruce Shelley, "Why Work," *Christianity Today,* July 14, 1987, p. 16.
2. J. P. Moreland, "Work, the Good Life and the Great Commission,"
   Worldwide Challenge, August 1988, p. 57.
3. Raymond C. Ortlund, *Lord, Make My Life a Miracle* (Glendale, Calif.:
   Regal, 1974), pp. 1-2.
4. Saint Augustine, *Confessions.*
5. John Piper, *Desiring God* (Portland, Oreg.: Multnomah, 1986), p. 41.
6. Ellen Fielding, "Career Change," *Christianity Today,* December 11,
   1987, p. 27.
7. David J. Frahm, *The Great Niche Hunt* (Colorado Springs, Colo.:
   NavPress, 1991), p. 28.
8. Henry T. Blackaby and Claude V. King, *Experiencing God* (Nashville,
   Tenn.: Broadman & Holman, 1994), p. 20.

9. Dee Brestin, *My Daughter, My Daughter* (Colorado Springs, Colo.: Chariot Victor, 1999), p. 41.

10. Elisabeth Elliot, *The Glory of God's Will* (Westchester, Ill.: Good News, 1982).

CHAPTER 5: WHY ME? WHY THIS? WHY NOW?

1. Philip Yancey, *Disappointment with God* (Grand Rapids, Mich.: Zondervan, 1988), pp. 44-46.

2. Stephen Olford quoted in a verbal presentation by Peg Rankin, Monmouth Beach, New Jersey.

3. Yancey, p. 152.

4. Adapted from Larry Crabb, *Inside Out* (Colorado Springs, Colo.: NavPress, 1988), p. 14.

CHAPTER 6: LORD, MAKE ME FLEXIBLE!

1. Jackie Hudson, *Doubt—A Road to Growth* (San Bernardino, Calif.: Here's Life, 1987), p. 20.

2. Tim Hansel, *You Gotta Keep Dancin'* (Elgin, Ill.: David C. Cook, 1985), p. 133.

CHAPTER 7: PLEASE HEAR ME!

1. Jan Fawcett, *Before It's Too Late,* prepared by the American Association of Suicidology (West Point, Penn.: Merek Sharp & Dohme), p. 7.

2. Elisabeth Elliot, *Loneliness* (Nashville: Oliver-Nelson, 1988), back cover.

3. C. S. Lewis, *The Four Loves,* quoted by Elisa Morgan, "Friendmaking," *Focal Point,* the quarterly of Denver Conservative Baptist Seminary.

CHAPTER 8: PLEASE HOLD ME!

1. Terri Schultz, "Does Marriage Give Women What They Really Want?" *Ladies Home Journal,* June 1980, p. 90.

2. M. Scott Peck, quoted by Robert J. Carlson, "Battling Sexual Indiscretion," *Ministry,* January 1987, pp. 4-6.

3. Marshall Shelley, "From the Editor," *Leadership,* Winter 1988, vol. IX, no. 1, p. 3.

4. Josh D. McDowell and Dick Day, *Why Wait? What You Need to Know About the Teen Sexuality Crisis* (San Bernardino, Calif.: Here's Life Publishers, 1987), p. 318.

5. Walter Trobisch, *I Loved a Girl* (New York: Harper & Row Publishers, 1965), pp. 3-4.

CHAPTER 9: I BLEW IT AGAIN!
1. Bob Benson, *Come Share the Being* (Nashville, Tenn.: Impact Books, 1974), pp. 72-73.
2. Philip Yancey, *Disappointment with God* (Grand Rapids, Mich.: Zondervan, 1988), p. 106.

CHAPTER 10: SELF-ACTUALIZATION?
1. Paraphrased in part from Polly Redford, *Raccoons and Eagles: Two Views of American Wildlife* (New York: E. P. Dutton, 1965), p. 191.
2. M. Scott Peck, *The Road Less Traveled: A New Psychology of Love, Traditional Values and Spiritual Growth* (New York: Simon and Schuster, 1978), p. 44.
3. Chris Thurman, *The Lies We Believe* (Nashville, Tenn.: Thomas Nelson, 1989), p. 58.

CHAPTER 11: WHATEVER THE ABUNDANT LIFE IS, I WANT IT!
1. Rusty Rustenbach, "What Do You Expect?" *Discipleship Journal,* no. 53, 1989, p. 59.

CHAPTER 12: ME—GOD'S WOMAN?
1. Cliff Barrows, quoted from a tribute in *Corrie ten Boom: Clippings from My Notebook* (Minneapolis: World Wide Publications, 1984), p. 3.
2. J. Oswald Sanders, *Spiritual Leadership* (Chicago: Moody Press, 1967), p. 40.

TWELVE-WEEK BIBLE STUDY
1. Emily Dickinson, *The Complete Poems of Emily Dickinson,* Thomas H. Johnson, ed., copyright 1960 by Mary L. Hampson (Boston: Little, Brown and Company, 1960), p. 133.
2. Sue Monk Kidd, *God's Joyful Surprise* (New York: Harper & Row, 1987), p. 3.
3. Carol Kent & Karen Lee-Thorp, *Six Steps to Clarify Your Calling* (Colorado Springs, Colo.: NavPress, 2000), pp. 21-22.
4. J. Oswald Sanders, *Spiritual Leadership* (Chicago: Moody Press, 1967), p. 40.

Laying down my Isacc

Author

CAROL KENT is the president of Speak Up Speaker Services, a Christian speakers' bureau, and the founder and director of Speak Up With Confidence seminars, a ministry committed to helping Christians develop their communication skills.

A member of the National Speakers Association, Carol is a nationally known speaker for conferences and retreats throughout the United States and Canada. A former radio show cohost, Carol has a B.S. in speech education and an M.A. in communication arts from Western Michigan University. She has been a featured speaker on *Focus on the Family* radio broadcasts and at the Praise Gathering for Believers. She has also been a keynoter for the Heritage Keepers and Time Out for Women arena events. She is a popular guest on a wide variety of radio and television programs and has been featured in a cover interview in *Today's Christian Woman* magazine.

Her books include *Becoming a Woman of Influence, Tame Your Fears, Speak Up with Confidence, Mothers Have Angel Wings,* and *Detours, Tow Trucks, and Angels in Disguise.* She has also cowritten the Designed for Influence Bible study series with Karen Lee-Thorp, along with the guided journal *My Soul's Journey: Becoming Who God Wants Me to Be* (all NavPress).

Carol and her husband, Gene, make their home in Port Huron, Michigan. They have one grown son and two granddaughters.

To schedule Carol Kent to speak for your next event, please contact Speak Up Speaker Services toll free at (888) 870-7719 or by e-mail at: Speakupinc@aol.com www.SpeakUpSpeakerServices.com

OVERCOME FEARS, DISCOVER YOUR INFLUENCE!

Tame Your Fears

Carol Kent examines ten fears common to most women and suggests ways to overcome such fears by using them as stepping stones to deeper faith, renewed confidence, and sincere reverence for a powerful and loving God.

by Carol Kent
1-57683-359-3

 ## Designed for Influence Series

Through the *Designed for Influence* series, authors Carol Kent and Karen Lee-Thorp encourage women to live out their God-designed purpose in six key areas. With the life of Christ as their model, the authors mentor women in the same way Jesus did—helping people live for things that last forever.

Six Keys to Lasting Friendships
1-57683-132-9

Six Choices That Will Change Your Life
1-57683-206-6

Six Basics of a Balanced Life
1-57683-135-3

Six Essentials of Spiritual Authenticity
1-57683-177-9

Six Secrets of a Confident Woman
1-57683-205-8

Six Steps to Clarify Your Calling
1-57683-203-1

To get your copies, visit your local bookstore, call 1-800-366-7788, or log on to www.navpress.com. Ask for a FREE catalog of NavPress products. Offer #BPA.

NAVPRESS

BRINGING TRUTH TO LIFE
www.navpress.com